Best Hikes Las Vegas

Best Hikes
Las Vegas

The Greatest Views, Wildlife, and Desert Strolls

Second Edition

Bruce Grubbs

GUILFORD, CONNECTICUT

To my parents, who got
me started in the outdoors
as soon as I could walk

FALCONGUIDES®

An imprint of The Rowman & Littlefield Publishing Group, Inc.
4501 Forbes Blvd., Ste. 200
Lanham, MD 20706
www.rowman.com

Falcon and FalconGuides are registered trademarks and Make Adventure Your Story is a trademark
of The Rowman & Littlefield Publishing Group, Inc.

Distributed by NATIONAL BOOK NETWORK

All photos by Bruce Grubbs unless otherwise noted
Maps by The Rowman & Littlefield Publishing Group, Inc.

British Library Cataloguing in Publication Information available

Library of Congress Control Number: 2020942016

ISBN 978-1-4930-5123-6 (paper : alk. paper)
ISBN 978-1-4930-5124-3 (electronic)

∞™ The paper used in this publication meets the minimum requirements of American National
Standard for Information Sciences—Permanence of Paper for Printed Library Materials, ANSI/NISO
Z39.48-1992.

Contents

The Hikes

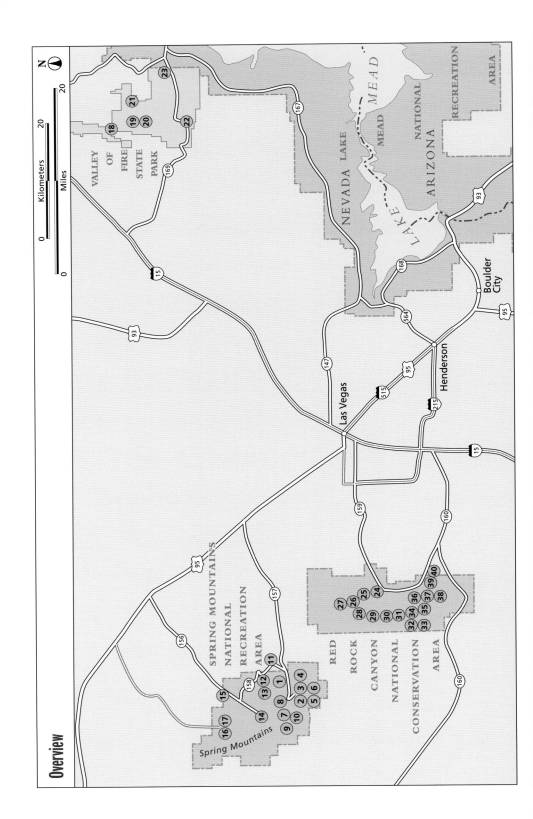

Overview

Acknowledgments

I'd like to thank Duart Martin for encouraging this project at every step and putting up with my absences while I mapped the trails and shot the photos. Thank you to Lee Kirkland, Red Rock Canyon National Conservation Area, for reviewing the manuscript. Thanks to my editors, John Burbidge and Mason Gadd, as well as Melissa Baker, map coordinator, for turning my rough manuscript into another polished FalconGuide.

From the summit of Cathedral Rock, you'll enjoy a panoramic view of Kyle Canyon, including the cliff-bound summit of Mummy Mountain.

conditions cause bristlecone pines to grow very slowly but in turn survive for thousands of years. The oldest tree on earth is found in the White Mountains just over the Nevada border in eastern California—the Methuselah Tree, a Great Basin bristlecone pine, is 4,851 years old.

Arctic Alpine

With the same climate as the polar regions of the planet, only low-growing plants can survive in the area between 11,000 and 12,000 feet. Lichen, a few grasses, and mat-like flowers such as phlox grow on and in sheltered areas among the rocks. But much of the landscape is bare rock and talus. The Mount Charleston Loop traverses several miles of this life zone.

Animals

The largest predator found in this area is the mountain lion, or cougar. Favoring remote mountain areas, mountain lions prey on deer and shy away from human contact. Most hikers are lucky to ever see a mountain lion's track, let alone the actual animal. Although mountain lions are usually not dangerous to humans, attacks have occurred in areas where human development encroaches on mountain lion habitat. Some such attacks have involved dogs running loose. If you encounter a mountain lion, keep children and pets with you and make yourself as large as possible while backing away slowly. Do not turn your back on the lion. If attacked, fight back aggressively with whatever weapons you have.

Mule deer are common throughout the area and especially in the mountains. They forage on plants at dawn and dusk. Coyotes prey on jackrabbits, cottontail rabbits, and small rodents and have adapted well to human presence. Their wild yipping is symbolic of the West, and they almost always sound closer than they are.

Wild horses and burros are found throughout Nevada, descended from domesticated animals set loose or lost by early prospectors and travelers. The Red Rock Scenic Drive and the Moenkopi Loop Trail in the Red Rock Canyon area are good places to see wild burros. Cold Creek Road in the Spring Mountains passes through a wild horse range.

Rattlesnakes strike fear into many first-time visitors to the desert. Found at all elevations except the very highest, the hazard can be minimized with some understanding of their habits. Rattlesnakes are cold-blooded reptiles and therefore are dependent on their environment to maintain themselves at a comfortable temperature. Contrary to popular belief, high temperatures quickly kill rattlesnakes. They prefer surfaces of about 80 degrees Fahrenheit. This means that they'll seek out shade or old burrows during hot, sunny weather. On the other hand, cool weather sends rattlesnakes

Paintbrush is a startling contrast against the early morning shadows.

to warm, sunny places such as rock slabs. That tells you where to watch for rattle-snakes as you hike. Another factor is that rattlesnakes can only strike about half their body length, so you should avoid placing your hands within about 3 feet of possible rattlesnake hangouts, such as shady rock overhangs.

Usually, rattlesnakes sense your presence through ground vibrations and move off without your being aware of them. If you do surprise one, or get too close, the unmistakable rattle comes into play. Stop, listen, and locate the snake before moving away. Rattlesnakes are not aggressive and will not give chase. Finally, rattlesnake venom is not the deadly poison of people's imagination. Very few victims die. The venom is tissue-destructive, and the snake's fangs are loaded with nasty bacteria, so the main danger from a bite is a nasty wound and possible infection. Most rattlesnake victims are snake collectors or people who were playing around with rattlesnakes. All that said, any snakebite victim should seek medical care as soon as possible.

Rattlesnakes, like their nonvenomous relatives, are a vital part of the wildlife community. They eat rodents and other small mammals and help keep their populations in check. Never kill or attempt to handle rattlesnakes or any other snake.

Certain spiders, including black widow and brown recluse spiders, can inflict dangerous bites. Both spiders like dark, secluded areas such as brush piles or the bases of clumps of brush. Once again, follow the desert rule of not placing your hands where you can't see them. Black widow spiders inject a neurotoxic venom, which causes difficult breathing and mild paralysis. Seek medical care if bitten. Brown recluse spiders aren't life-threatening, but the bites tend to develop into nasty wounds that take a long time to heal.

You'll sometimes spot tarantulas crossing roads or trails during their migrations. Although sometimes 3 or 4 inches across, these fearsome-looking, hairy spiders are not dangerous.

The most deadly animal, at least at lower desert elevations, is the common bark scorpion, although the main danger is to the very young or elderly. Once again, knowing their habits will almost eliminate scorpion stings. Bark scorpions come out to hunt insects at night, and spend their days clinging upside down beneath rocks, sticks, or bark. To avoid nasty encounters, never place your hands where you can't see them, never walk around in the desert barefoot, use a flashlight when moving around camp at night, and always kick rocks and sticks over before picking them up.

Respect all wildlife by staying at a safe distance. Use a telephoto lens for photography. Never feed any wild animal. Animals get dependent on handouts, and then starve during the winter when their human benefactors are not around. So instead of helping them, you're actually hurting wild animals by feeding them.

Birds

Although there are many species of birds in this area, some of the most common are piñon jays, which are found in large flocks in the piñon-juniper woodland. Their quiet peeping twitter is symbolic of the piñon-juniper woodland. These dusty blue birds forage for pine nuts during the summer and hide them in caches to use during the winter.

Ravens and crows are everywhere. These intelligent birds will eat just about anything, but they're usually seen scavenging roadkill and food scraps. Red-tailed hawks are commonly seen resting on fence posts or soaring above the desert valleys and slopes, hunting for small rodents. Steller's jays have a distinctive blue crest on their heads and can be heard noisily defending their territories among the tall ponderosa pines. Up among the bristlecone pines, you'll see another jay, Clark's nutcracker, which is hard to miss with its black, gray, and white color scheme. They are also known as camp robbers because of their bold attempts to score dropped food.

Prehistory

Current evidence shows that the first humans in Nevada arrived about 13,000 years ago. Large animals such as horses, elephants, and camels shared the valleys and the mountains with these early humans. Archaeological excavations at Tule Springs, about 15 miles northwest of Las Vegas, show that this was man's first known settlement in Nevada, about 12,400 years ago.

The climate was much wetter 10,000 years ago than it is at present. Two huge lakes occupied the valleys of northwestern Nevada (Lake Lahontan) and northeastern Nevada (Lake Bonneville). In southern Nevada the forests extended much lower down the mountainsides, and the desert valley of Las Vegas was probably a piñon-juniper woodland. Fish, land animals, and food plants would have been much more

There are three main panels and several smaller panels of petroglyphs along the Mouse's Tank Trail. Petroglyphs are pecked into the rock.

plentiful then. With the relative plenty and milder climate, more advanced societies developed, especially along the ancient lakeshores.

Rock art dating from 5,000 to 7,000 years ago is common in Nevada, especially along migratory game trails and in areas where people once congregated. There are fine examples of petroglyphs (rock art pecked into the rock) along Petroglyph Canyon in Valley of Fire State Park.

When the Escalante-Domínguez expedition passed through southern Nevada in 1776, the Native Americans they encountered were Southern Paiutes. Nomadic hunter-gatherers, the Southern Paiutes traveled in small bands or extended family units of up to fifty people. Occasional bands would gather to form temporary villages of hundreds of people, especially in the fall in areas where the piñon nut harvest was good. But resources were too scarce to support permanent villages in the post-glacial Great Basin and Mohave Deserts.

History

The first non-native known to have entered southern Nevada was a Spanish missionary named Francisco Garcés. In 1776 he traveled up the lower Colorado River past the rock formations he named the "Needles," a few miles south of the present town of Needles, California. It appears that he traveled a few miles into the very southern tip of Nevada.

Peter Skene Ogden, a fur trapper, barely made it into the northeast corner of the state in 1826. In the same year, Jedediah Strong Smith crossed the southern tip of the state and established a campsite near some springs in the broad valley east of the Spring Mountains. This camp, Las Vegas, would become a major stop along the Old Spanish Trail. He entered the state near the present town of Mesquite and traveled along Meadow Valley Wash and the Virgin River. Smith named the Virgin River the Adams River for John Quincy Adams, although the name didn't stick.

Reports brought back by the early fur traders and explorers, although often inaccurate and embellished, increased the nation's interest in the American West. The federal government sent a number of official survey parties to the West to explore and create accurate maps. In 1843 Captain John C. Frémont was sent west and began his explorations in northern Nevada. In 1844 Frémont followed the Old Spanish Trail westward to Las Vegas and then continued east into Utah via the Virgin River.

Frémont named many features during his explorations of Nevada, and came up with the term "Great Basin" to describe the intermountain area of the West, including nearly all of Nevada, that has no outlet to the sea.

Few emigrant parties crossed Nevada before the California gold rush began in 1848. When the trickle became a flood, most parties used routes across the northern part of the state, such as the Humboldt River, which has more water sources. The hazards of the route through southern Nevada were made famous by the experiences of the Manly-Bennett party. This group traveled a route north of the Spring Mountains, crossed the Amargosa Desert, and descended into Death Valley, where heat and lack of water trapped the main body.

Reports from the early explorers and prospectors made clear the potential for ranching and farming in the broad valleys of Nevada. Quite a few large ranches were established in the 1860s. Mountain streams and springs were diverted for irrigation, and the discovery of plentiful groundwater under many of the valleys led to the digging and drilling of wells. Most of the crops were grown to provide winter feed for livestock, though some human food crops were grown as well. Ranches had to be large, as the sparse natural forage required vast amounts of land to feed cattle. Much of the rangeland used by cattle is public land, and today the ranchers pay a fee to the federal government in order to graze their animals. Even today the major economic activity in fourteen of Nevada's sixteen counties is ranching and farming.

The Las Vegas area was settled by Mormon expeditions sent from Salt Lake City. In addition to Las Vegas, Mormon settlers established a number of other towns in southern Nevada, including Callville on the Colorado River (now under Lake Mead).

As more people moved into the state, transportation in Nevada gradually improved. The trappers and prospectors mostly traveled on horse- or mule-back, trailing pack trains to haul supplies, furs, and ore. Emigrant trains generally used wagons pulled by oxen, though most members of the party usually walked. As mining camps and towns became established, the need for heavy transport increased. Freight companies hauled supplies and ore with heavy wagons pulled by a dozen or more animals (such as the famous "twenty-mule team"). The coming of the first railroad across the state, the Union Pacific of Golden Spike fame, in 1869 marked a revolution in travel. A journey that took weeks or months by horse or stage became a comfortable trip of a few days. Spur railroads were rapidly built to the major mining centers and settlements.

Nevada was originally part of the Spanish colonies in the New World, though the Spanish had little to do with the area. After the Mexican Revolution in 1822, Nevada was part of Mexico until the Treaty of Guadalupe Hidalgo in 1848 ceded California, Nevada, New Mexico, and most of Arizona to the United States. For a couple of years, Nevada was part of the Mormon "State of Deseret," but Congress soon designated the Territory of Utah, which included Nevada until it became a separate territory in 1860. Nevada became a state in 1864.

The rapid population growth that made it possible for Nevada to achieve statehood relatively quickly was caused in large part by the discovery of gold and silver in western Nevada. News of the rich Comstock Lode at Virginia City attracted a flood of prospectors, miners, shopkeepers, and teamsters, as well as more farmers and ranchers, who sold food to the mining towns. Since then mining has been a major part of Nevada's economy, though the inevitable boom-and-bust cycle that follows changes in prices and world markets makes life unpredictable for mining communities.

Hoover Dam on the Colorado River, which was constructed between 1931 and 1936, was the world's first large reclamation dam. Its primary purposes were to control the erratic flows of the Colorado River, which ranged from a trickle in late

Ponderosa pine is the largest tree in the Spring Mountains and is easily identified by its 5- to 7-inch needles that grow in clusters of three.

summer to raging floods during the spring snowmelt in the Rocky Mountains, and to generate electric power. It was this nearby source of cheap hydroelectric power that made the growth of Las Vegas possible.

After 1945, tourism and gambling grew rapidly and are to this day a major part of the economy—especially in the Reno and Las Vegas areas. With the rise of Native American gaming in many states, Las Vegas has had to reinvent itself as a diverse entertainment center. Although most visitors come to Las Vegas for the casinos and the shows, a portion of those visitors seek out the nearby natural areas, as do locals.

Place Names

Although Native Americans certainly had names for all the geographic features with which they came in contact, the lack of a written language meant that the only means of preserving these place names was by oral tradition. Still, some Native American place names survived long enough to be recorded by European explorers. Among the newcomers who attached names to geographic features, as well as man-made features such as towns and roads, were the early fur trappers and explorers, emigrant trains, prospectors and miners, traders, stage and freight line operators, the railroad builders, and government surveyors, agencies, and officials.

Official place names, as designated by the US Board on Geographic Names and recorded in the Geographic Names Information System (GNIS) database, are used throughout this book. Local, informal names are used when there is no official name. The GNIS database is also the source for the summit elevations in the book. A recent resurvey of summit elevations using the latest advances in surveying methods has resulted in changes in many summit elevations. The result is that elevations shown on maps and mentioned in the text of this book are often different than the elevations used in older books and shown on US Geological Survey (CalTopo.com MapBuilder Topo layer; USGS) topographic maps.

Wilderness Restrictions and Regulations

At present, permits are not required for any of the hikes in this book, whether day hiking or backpacking. There are regulations specific to each area.

Spring Mountains National Recreation Area

Campfires are not allowed at any time of year within the three wilderness areas: Mount Charleston, La Madre, and Rainbow Wildernesses. Backpackers must use camp stoves. From April 15 to November 15, campfires are allowed only in fire pits and grills provided within USDA Forest Service–developed campgrounds. Motor vehicles are not allowed on trails within the NRA and are not allowed in wilderness areas. All litter and trash must be packed out or placed in trash containers. Historic and archaeological sites are protected by federal law and must not be damaged or disturbed.

Valley of Fire State Park

Campfires are allowed only in the grills and fire pits provided within the developed campgrounds. Dogs must be on leashes no longer than 6 feet. Motor vehicles are not permitted on any trail and must be operated only on designated roads. All litter and trash must be packed out or placed in trash containers. Plants, animals, and all other natural features as well as cultural and archaeological sites are protected by state and federal law and must not be damaged or disturbed.

Red Rock Canyon National Conservation Area

Camping is permitted only in the designated campgrounds. Campfires are allowed only in the grills and fire pits provided in the campgrounds. Motor vehicles are not permitted on any trail and must be operated only on designated roads. All litter and trash must be packed out or placed in trash containers. Plants, animals, and all other

Although the official name of the red rock cliffs at Red Rock Canyon is Sandstone Bluffs, the local and much more descriptive name is Red Rock Escarpment.

natural features as well as cultural and archaeological sites are protected by federal law and must not be damaged or disturbed.

About Wildfires

In recent years some of the mountains and deserts near Las Vegas have suffered a number of unusually large and destructive wildfires. While fire has always been part of the ecology in Nevada, a combination of drought, invasion by exotic grasses and other plants, tree-killing insect epidemics, and over-dense forests caused by more than a century of poor management practices has led to unusually intense fires not only in the forests but in the desert as well. Some of the hikes in this book have been affected by recent fires, and more will be affected in the future. Always call or e-mail the land management agency before your hike, or at least check their website, for current conditions and possible area or trail closures.

Quaking aspens are the first trees to return to an old burn on the North Loop Trail below Mummy Mountain.

How to Use This Guide

Start: Directions to all the trailheads begin from downtown Las Vegas at the intersection of US 95 and I-15, and the total distance from this point to the trailhead is listed here.

Distance: This is the total distance of the hike, whether out and back, around a loop, or one way with a car shuttle. Distances were measured with computer mapping software and websites. Although slightly shorter than distances measured on the ground with a trail wheel, the mileages are consistent throughout the book.

Approximate hiking time: The time for an average hiker to do the hike. These times err on the conservative side but do not take into account rest stops, photography, and other non-hiking activities. Fast hikers will need less time, while slow or out-of-shape hikers may use more time.

Difficulty: All hikes are rated as easy, moderate, or strenuous, with reasons for the rating. Although this is necessarily a highly subjective rating, nearly anyone who can walk should be able to do an easy hike in just a few hours. Moderate hikes are longer—up to a full day—and may involve several hundred feet or more of elevation gain, and possibly cross-country hiking as well. Experienced hikers will have no problems; beginners should hike with someone more experienced and will have more fun if they are in reasonable shape. Strenuous hikes are very long, requiring a full day of hiking by fit hikers, or several days in the case of backpack trips. The hiking may involve cross-country or faint, rough trails that require good map and compass skills, and some rock scrambling may be required on rough terrain. Only fit, experienced hikers should tackle these hikes.

Trail surface: Most trails in the Las Vegas region are dirt and rocks. Other trail surface conditions are described here, including hikes on old roads, paved trails, and cross-country.

Best season: The best part of the year to do the hike, taking into account such conditions as winter snow and summer heat.

Water: For backpackers and for emergency use by day hikers, this section lists known water sources. Most springs and creeks should be considered seasonal, and you should never depend on a single source of water. All water should be purified before using it to drink or cook. Day hikers should carry all the water they'll need.

Other trail users: You may encounter horses and/or mountain bikes on some of the trails.

Canine compatibility: Many people like to hike with their furry friends, so this section mentions whether dogs are allowed, and restrictions, if any. All areas that are open to dogs require that they be under control, which for most dogs means on a leash. If your dog barks or runs up to other hikers, even in a friendly way, then it is not under control and must be kept on a leash. This is just common courtesy to other hikers, some of whom may have had bad experiences with dogs.

Fees and permits: If any fees, including entry fees, are required, they are mentioned here. Any permits required are also listed.

Schedule: If access is limited to certain times of the day for administrative reasons such as road closures, you'll find that information here.

Maps: The CalTopo.com MapBuilder Topo layer and the USGS 7.5-minute series quads covering the hike are listed here, but note that trails are usually out of date or not shown on the USGS maps. Nevertheless, the USGS maps are the most accurate maps for depicting the terrain. Valley of Fire State Park is the only area in this book covered by a National Geographic Trails Illustrated map, but that map, Lake Mead National Recreation Area, does not show trails in the state park. The best trail map for the area covered by this book are the MapBuilder Topo and MapBuilder Hybrid layers in CalTopo's excellent web- and app-based digital maps (CalTopo .com). You can print custom maps for the area of your hike including any of the topo, street mapping, and satellite and aerial image layers. Gaia GPS (GaiaGPS.com) is another excellent digital map app and website.

Trail contacts: Look here for the name and contact information of the agency or organization responsible for managing the land crossed by the hike. It's a good idea to call or e-mail the land-management agency before your hike to check on road and trail conditions. Where possible, the contact information includes the mailing and street address, phone number, and website. E-mail addresses are not included because they change frequently; check the agency website for an e-mail address, generally found under a "Contact" link. Sometimes web addresses change as well, but you can usually find land-management units on the web with a search engine.

Special considerations: This section lists unusual conditions that may exist for the hike.

Finding the trailhead: This section gives driving directions from the intersection of US 95 and I-15 in downtown Las Vegas, as well as the GPS coordinates in latitude and longitude.

The Hike: Here's the meat of the hike—a detailed description of the trail or route and the features and attractions along the way. I describe the route using landmarks as well as trail signs, when possible, because trail signs can be missing. Refer to the next section, "Miles and Directions," for a description with distances between key points.

Miles and Directions: This table lists the key points, such as trail intersections, or turning points on a cross-country hike, by miles and tenths. You should be able to find the route with this table alone. The mileages in this book do not necessarily agree with

White fir appears toward the top of the ponderosa pine forest on the slopes of the mountains, and has flattened single needles with a whitish stripe.

distances found on trail signs, agency mileages, and other descriptions, because trail miles are measured by a variety of methods and personnel. All mileages were carefully measured using digital topographic mapping software for accuracy and consistency within the book.

Green Tips: As you take advantage of the spectacular scenery offered by the Las Vegas area, remember that our planet is very dear, very special, and very fragile. All of us should do everything we can to keep it clean, beautiful, and healthy, including following the Green Tips you'll find throughout this book.

Trail Finder

Hike No.	Hike Name	Best Hikes for Backpackers	Best Hikes for Waterfalls	Best Hikes for Geology Lovers	Best Hikes for Children	Best Hikes for Dogs	Best Hikes for Peak Baggers	Best Hikes for Great Views	Best Hikes for Canyons	Best Hikes for Nature Lovers
1	Fletcher Canyon			•	•	•				
2	Echo Trail				•	•			•	
3	Little Falls		•		•	•			•	
4	Cathedral Rock			•			•	•		
5	Griffith Peak			•			•	•		
6	Charleston Peak via South Loop Trail	•					•	•		•
7	Mummy Spring via Trail Canyon			•						•
8	Charleston Peak via Trail Canyon	•		•			•			
9	Mary Jane Falls		•	•				•		•
10	Big Falls		•	•					•	
11	Robbers Roost			•	•	•				•
12	Fletcher Peak			•			•	•		
13	Mummy Spring via North Loop Trail			•						•
14	Bristlecone Loop					•		•		•

Hike No.	Hike Name	Best Hikes for Backpackers	Best Hikes for Waterfalls	Best Hikes for Geology Lovers	Best Hikes for Children	Best Hikes for Dogs	Best Hikes for Peak Baggers	Best Hikes for Great Views	Best Hikes for Canyons	Best Hikes for Nature Lovers
15	Sawmill Loop				•	•				•
16	Bonanza Peak						•	•		
17	Bonanza Trail	•						•		
18	White Domes Loop			•					•	•
19	Rainbow Vista Trail			•					•	•
20	Petroglyph Canyon				•	•			•	•
21	Silica Dome			•			•	•		
22	Arrowhead Trail					•		•		
23	Elephant Rock Loop			•		•		•		•
24	Moenkopi Loop				•	•		•		•
25	Calico Hills			•	•	•				
26	Calico Tanks			•					•	•
27	Turtlehead Mountain			•			•			
28	Keystone Thrust			•				•		
29	White Rock Hills Overlook			•		•		•		
30	Willow Spring Loop				•					•
31	La Madre Spring									•
32	North Peak			•			•	•		

Hike No.	Hike Name	Best Hikes for Backpackers	Best Hikes for Waterfalls	Best Hikes for Geology Lovers	Best Hikes for Children	Best Hikes for Dogs	Best Hikes for Peak Baggers	Best Hikes for Great Views	Best Hikes for Canyons	Best Hikes for Nature Lovers
33	Bridge Mountain			•			•	•		
34	White Rock–Willow Spring Trail					•				
35	Lost Creek Loop–Children's Discovery Trail		•		•				•	•
36	Base of the Escarpment	•		•				•		
37	Icebox Canyon		•		•				•	
38	Pine Creek Canyon								•	•
39	Oak Creek Canyon					•			•	•
40	First Creek Canyon					•			•	•

Map Legend

Transportation

≡⟨15⟩≡   Interstate Highway

≡⟨95⟩≡   US Highway

≡(169)≡   State Highway

≡⟨1431⟩≡   Other Road

= = = =   Unpaved Road

Trails

------   Selected Route

------   Trail or Fire Road

········   Cross-country Route

——→   Direction of Travel

Water Features

Body of Water

Intermittent Stream

Waterfall

Land Management

Local & State Parks

National Forest &
Wilderness Areas

Symbols

①   Trailhead

Bridge

■   Building/Point of Interest

▲   Campground

∩   Cave

▲   Mountain/Peak

🅿   Parking

Pass

🅰   Picnic Area

🚻   Restroom

◄   Scenic View

○   Towns and Cities

🚻   Restroom

❓   Visitor Center

Spring Mountains

By far the most dramatic mountain range in southern Nevada, the Spring Mountains rise nearly 2 miles above the surrounding desert valleys and reach 11,811 feet at Charleston Peak. From this and other 11,000-foot summits in the range, the view extends more than 200 miles, often including the 14,000-foot Sierra Nevada in California. The range starts near the California border and runs 80 miles to the north and northwest, forming the western skyline for Las Vegas.

Charleston Peak, flanked by the ridges above Kyle Canyon, is seen from Griffith Peak.

GREEN TIP:
When hiking with your dog, stay in the center of the path and keep Fido close by. Dogs that run loose can harm fragile soils and spread pesky plants by carrying their seeds. Never let your dog run up to other hikers, no matter how friendly it is. Some people have had bad experiences with dogs and do not appreciate dogs running up to them.

The Spring Mountains have long been the summer retreat for the desert dwellers of Las Vegas and other nearby towns. While the desert cities roast in summer heat of over 100 degrees Fahrenheit, the peaks, canyons, and trails of the Spring Mountains are as much as 50 degrees cooler. And in the winter, heavy snowfall makes winter recreation possible, including cross-country skiing and snowshoeing. Many of the trails in this book are great winter snowshoeing routes.

The Spring Mountains were named for the numerous springs that occur through-out the range. Known to locals as the Mount Charleston area, the Spring Mountains cover a much larger area than most people realize. Although smaller ranges and areas such as the La Madre Mountains and Red Rock Canyon area are actually part of the Spring Mountains, this section focuses on the portion included in the Spring Mountains National Recreation Area, which is the northwestern section containing the highest peaks. Just to clear up some confusion, "Mount Charleston" is the name of the village at the head of Kyle Canyon, while the summit of the range is Charleston Peak. Kyle Canyon is such a dramatic location, with its towering limestone cliffs, that many people assume that glaciers carved this deep canyon. Actually, there's no evidence of glacial activity in the Spring Mountains, but the mountains still have an alpine aspect that is especially appealing in contrast to the surrounding desert. It's all part of the contrasts that make hiking around Las Vegas so great.

1 Fletcher Canyon

This hike starts just down the road from the Spring Mountains Visitor Center and is a perfect first hike for those new to the Spring Mountains. It features a beautiful forested canyon, a seasonal spring, a narrow limestone slot canyon, and wilderness solitude—all within 2.0 miles of the busy Kyle Canyon Road.

Start: 37.0 miles northwest of Las Vegas
Distance: 3.6 miles out and back
Approximate hiking time: 2 hours
Difficulty: Moderate due to 770-foot elevation change
Trail surface: Dirt and rocks, some steep sections of unmaintained trail, and some rock scrambling beyond Fletcher Spring
Best seasons: Spring through fall
Water: Fletcher Spring

Other trail users: Horses
Canine compatibility: Leashed dogs permitted
Fees and permits: None
Schedule: Open all hours
Maps: USGS Angel Peak
Trail contacts: Spring Mountains National Recreation Area, Humboldt-Toiyabe National Forest, 4701 N. Torrey Pines Dr., Las Vegas 89130-2301; (702) 872-5486; https://www.fs.usda.gov/htnf

Finding the trailhead: From the intersection of US 95 and I-15 in downtown Las Vegas, drive northwest on US 95 16.7 miles. Turn left on NV 157, the Kyle Canyon Road. Continue 18.0 miles to the trailhead on the right side of the highway. There is additional parking along the left side of the highway. GPS: N36 15.813'/W115 36.699'

The Hike

Follow the Fletcher Canyon Trail through open stands of mixed ponderosa pine, piñon pine, and juniper into the open mouth of Fletcher Canyon. Along the first 100 yards of the trail, you may notice a lack of underbrush and small trees. This is because of an ongoing USDA Forest Service thinning project that is taking place along the upper portion of the Kyle Canyon Road. Crews are removing brush and small trees to reduce the intensity of wildfires along the highway. Popular roads such as this one are common points of origin for fires due to careless people throwing cigarettes and other burning material out of their cars. In steep terrain such as Kyle Canyon, wildfires can quickly grow in size and rate of spread as the fire encounters steeper slopes and heavier vegetation. Logs, brush, and small trees burn especially fast. In the right conditions Kyle Canyon could act like a chimney, directing an intense wildfire up the canyon and endangering people and structures. Since the best way to prevent a wildfire from becoming large and difficult to control is to catch it while it's small, the

▶ Never camp near an isolated spring or water source. Aside from the possibility of contamination due to human activity, your presence prevents wildlife from getting to the water.

Mature ponderosa pines can be found along the Fletcher Canyon Trail. These pines can reach 600 years in age.

thinning project aims to reduce the amount of fuel along the highway so that crews can build control lines and contain fires.

The trail crosses the dry streambed and stays on the north side of the drainage, climbing steadily. After you pass the signed wilderness boundary, watch for sections of the old pipeline that brought water down the canyon from Fletcher Spring. At a point where a trickle of water sometimes surfaces, the canyon narrows and the trail crosses to the south side and does several short, steep climbs. The maintained trail ends at Fletcher Spring, but you can walk on up the bed through an impressive narrows in the limestone. The walls tower 100 to 200 feet above the bed, and narrow to as little as 5 feet wide. A few easy scrambles lead over chockstones in the streambed. You'll come to a slightly more open spot where a side canyon comes in from the left. Stay right and climb the last hundred yards to a seasonal waterfall.

Springs such as Fletcher Spring are a vital source of water for wildlife in areas such as the Spring Mountains, where most creeks are seasonal. Early explorers also depended on these isolated water sources, and knowledge of "water holes" was essential for safe travel across the Nevada desert. The first European explorers hired native guides to help them find water. Emigrant wagon trains in turn hired mountain men and other explorers to guide them.

When people started to settle in places such as the Spring Mountains, they developed many of the springs to provide water for themselves and their domesticated animals. Often springs were dug out to provide a more reliable flow and then piped to a watering trough. In other cases pipelines were built to bring water to a homestead. Sections of the pipeline that once carried water from Fletcher Spring down to Kyle Canyon are still present along the trail. Such water projects required constant maintenance. Plant debris and sediment tended to clog the pipe intake at the spring, and freezing weather could break the pipeline. Floods are common in these mountain during the current date and time. Winter and spring are the best times to see the stars from Valley of Fire, while summer and fall are perfect times to look at the evening sky from a camp in the Spring Mountains.

Miles and Directions

0.0 From the trailhead, climb the stairs above the parking lot and turn right on the Echo Trail.

0.1 Stay right at an unsigned junction and cross the drainage.

0.2 Stay right at a road junction.

0.3 Stay left at a road junction.

0.6 Return the way you came.

1.2 Arrive back at the Lower Cathedral Trailhead..

The craggy summits of Cockscomb Ridge loom above the Echo Trail.

STARGAZING

The Milky Way is a band of light across the entire sky composed of millions of stars that are too faint to see with the naked eye. These stars make up the Milky Way galaxy, of which our sun is a member star. When looking at the Milky Way, you are literally looking at our home galaxy edge on.

From ancient times, humans have found patterns in the stars. Today eighty-eight constellations are recognized, covering the entire sky. All stars and other objects are found within one of these constellations, which in modern usage define a precise region of the sky. About half the constellations are major, made up of bright stars in a easily recognizable pattern. Learning the major constellations is the first step to knowing your way around the night sky. Here are a few of the major constellations to look for during a summer night at around 9 p.m.

Ursa Major, the Great Bear: Look north to find the Big Dipper, a group of stars that make up a dipper hanging from its handle with the bowl pointing right. The Big Dipper is an asterism—a named group of stars within the Great Bear constellation. The two stars at the right edge of the dipper are the Pointer Stars. A line drawn to the right through the Pointer Stars passes through Polaris, the North Star. In turn the North Star forms the end of the handle of the Little Dipper, part of the constellation Little Bear. The Little Dipper is much smaller and fainter than the Big Dipper.

Cassiopeia: To the right and below the North Star is a bright group of stars forming a sideways W in the sky.

Lyra: Nearly overhead in the summer sky, Lyra is a small but bright constellation representing a lyre, an ancient stringed musical instrument. A nearly perfect triangle shares one star with a parallelogram. The very bright star at one point of the triangle is Vega, one of the brightest stars in the sky.

Sagittarius, the Archer: In the southern sky, near the horizon, look for a group of bright stars forming an almost-perfect teapot, complete with handle, lid, and spout.

Scorpius, the Scorpion: Just to the right of Sagittarius, a large group of stars looks like a huge scorpion, with a bright pair of stars on the left making up the stinger, and a small group of fainter stars on the upper right representing the head. The bright red star in the middle of the constellation is Antares, a giant red star that is the heart of the scorpion.

Meteors, or "shooting stars," are small pieces of rock that enter our atmosphere from space at tremendous speeds. The streak of light is the object burning up in the atmosphere.

Most meteors are the size of a speck of sand, but occasionally a larger one will create a spectacular "fireball." While meteors can be seen every night from dark locations when the sky is clear, meteor showers appear at certain times of the year; the show may include dozens or even hundreds of meteors per hour. The best meteor showers are the Perseids in August, the Orionids in October, the Leonids in November, and the Geminids in December.

Five planets are visible to the naked eye: Mercury, Venus, Mars, Jupiter, and Saturn. Even small binoculars will show you the phases of Venus, the red color of Mars, the moons of Jupiter, and the rings of Saturn. Because the planets orbit the sun at various speeds, they appear to move across the sky, but always along the ecliptic, the plane of the solar system.

There are thousands of artificial satellites orbiting the earth, and many are easily seen by the naked eye. The best time to observe satellites is just after dusk, when the observer is in the dark but sunlight still strikes the satellites high overhead. Lie on your back and let your gaze wander over a broad patch of sky, looking for a "star" that moves. Some satellites, such as the Iridium series and the International Space Station, are very bright and are in low orbits that cause them to move quickly across the sky.

3 Little Falls

Little Falls is the smallest of the named waterfalls in Kyle Canyon and the easiest to reach. As with most of the waterfalls in the Spring Mountains, Little Falls is seasonal and is at its best during the spring snowmelt after a snowy winter in the high country.

Start: 37.5 miles northwest of Las Vegas
Distance: 0.8 mile out and back
Approximate hiking time: 30 minutes
Difficulty: Easy due to short distance and little elevation gain
Trail surface: Dirt and rocks
Best seasons: Spring through fall
Water: None
Other trail users: Horses
Canine compatibility: Leashed dogs permitted

Fees and permits: None
Schedule: Open all hours
Maps: USGS Mount Charleston
Trail contacts: Spring Mountains National Recreation Area, Humboldt-Toiyabe National Forest, 4701 N. Torrey Pines Dr., Las Vegas 89130-2301; (702) 872-5486; https://www.fs.usda.gov/htnf
Special considerations: The falls are best in the spring during snowmelt.

Finding the trailhead: From the intersection of US 95 and I-15 in downtown Las Vegas, drive 16.7 miles northwest on US 95. Turn left on NV 157, Kyle Canyon Road, and drive 20.8 miles to the Lower Cathedral Trailhead, on the right. Parking is limited, so it is best to arrive early, especially on weekends. There is additional parking in the Cathedral Rock Picnic Area just up the road. Entry to the picnic area requires a fee. GPS: N36 15.455' / W115 38.974'

The Hike

From the Lower Cathedral Trailhead, follow the Echo Trail to the west. When the trail turns right and descends slightly to cross a drainage, stay left on the unmarked Little Falls Trail. This trail stays left of the drainage and climbs steadily toward the imposing limestone cliffs ahead. Another sign that you're on the correct trail is the old pipeline that was used to tap the spring at the base of Little Falls. The falls themselves appear as the canyon narrows to a cul-de-sac.

Waterfalls are a short-lived feature of the landscape, geologically speaking. Rivers and streams, using the erosive power of water and gravity, try to create a smooth gradient, or steepness, along their path from headwaters to sea. The gradient is steepest at the headwaters, in this case the heads of the drainages in Kyle Canyon. The gradient gradually flattens as a stream descends the mountain slopes and becomes even flatter in the valleys. As a river nears the ocean, the gradient becomes very shallow as the waters of the river merge with the sea.

Anything that interrupts this ideal gradient is attacked by the stream and removed. If a lake forms along a stream because of some event such as a landslide, the lake forms a new base for the stream above, and it begins regrading itself in relation

As you climb, the towering limestone cliffs of Cathedral Rock loom above the trail to the west. Watch for a short unmarked spur trail to the left, at the end of one of the switchbacks. This trail leads to a small, pleasant, unnamed spring, one of the many hidden springs that gave the Spring Mountains their name. As the trail climbs to a point nearly level with the saddle south of Cathedral Rock, a final switchback leads to the right and traverses through a fine mixed stand of ponderosa pine, white fir, and Douglas fir. A second spring pours out of a culvert at the saddle.

Above the saddle the Cathedral Rock Trail makes its final ascent to the summit via a series of switchbacks. Because Cathedral Rock is at the end of a ridge projecting north, the views of Kyle Canyon are spectacular, extending the length of the canyon and far out into the desert to the east. To the south the long, high ridge that connects Griffith Peak and Charleston Peak, known locally as the South Rim, dominates the skyline high above you, with Charleston Peak visible to the southwest.

Many people assume that Kyle Canyon was carved by glaciers because of the imposing limestone cliffs. Actually, there is no evidence of glacial activity in the Spring Mountains. This spectacular landscape was carved primarily by flowing water. Since most of the streams are seasonal, much of the erosion takes place during the occasional major storm. Summer thunderstorms are especially effective at eroding

Charleston Peak on the left and the "North Rim" sit at the head of Kyle Canyon.

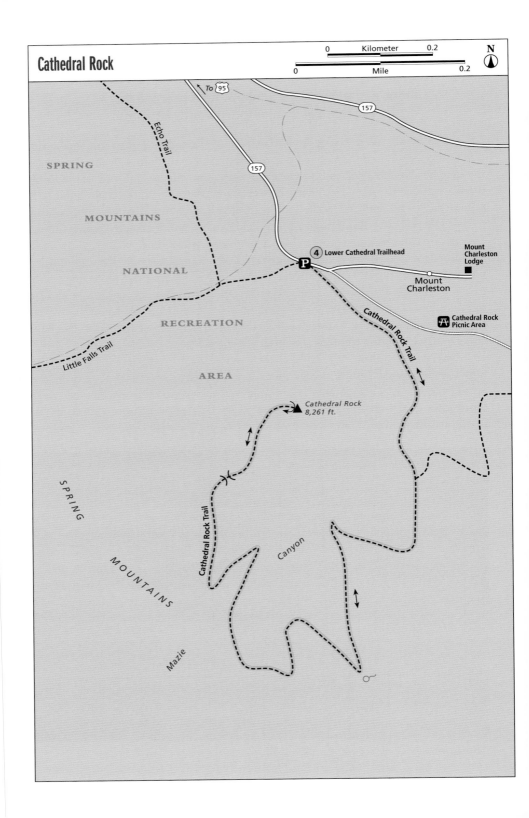

Cathedral Rock

0 | Kilometer | 0.2
0 | Mile | 0.2

N

To 95

157

157

SPRING

MOUNTAINS

NATIONAL

RECREATION

AREA

Echo Trail

Little Falls Trail

4 Lower Cathedral Trailhead

P

Mount Charleston

Mount Charleston Lodge

Cathedral Rock Picnic Area

Cathedral Rock Trail

Cathedral Rock 8,261 ft.

Cathedral Rock Trail

SPRING

MOUNTAINS

Mazie

Canyon

WILDFIRE PREVENTION

Although recent dry years and increasing numbers of recreationists visiting the mountains have caused the USDA Forest Service to ban campfires in the Spring Mountains during the warm half of the year, the ponderosa pine forests that grow at middle elevations used to be naturally resistant to fire. Look closely at the bark of a mature, yellow-barked ponderosa pine and you'll see that it is made up of layers of thin, puzzle-like pieces. These layers serve to insulate the living cambium beneath them from fire running up the tree and allow it to survive low-intensity ground fires. Such low-intensity fires were the norm before European settlers modified the forest through cattle grazing, logging, and fire suppression. As a result the ponderosa stands are denser now and there is more accumulated fuel on the forest floor. Fires tend to burn hotter and crown out—that is, get into the treetops. These hotter fires kill the trees and may even sterilize the soil. Such fires are especially dangerous in areas with a wildland-urban interface, such as Kyle Canyon.

One response to the situation is to thin trees and remove underbrush in an attempt to restore the forest to a more natural, fire-resistant condition. You can see the results of these efforts along the Kyle Canyon Road on the approach to the Cathedral Rock hike.

canyons because they commonly drop large amounts of rain into small areas in a short period of time. The resulting flash floods often contain more sand and rock than water and can cause dramatic changes in the landscape in a few hours.

The limestone formations in Kyle Canyon and the Spring Mountains are about the same age as the Redwall Limestone in the Grand Canyon. Massive limestone cliffs are common throughout the Rocky Mountains and intermountain areas of North America. The nearly pure limestone was deposited in a deep ocean environment. Microscopic sea creatures swam in this ancient ocean, and when they died their shells fell to the seafloor in a steady rain. Over millions of years the shells built up layers of sediment hundreds or even thousands of feet thick. As additional sediment accumulated on top, the layers of shells were compressed into solid rock.

Miles and Directions

0.0 Climb the stairs above the parking lot and turn left onto the Cathedral Rock Trail.

0.3 The trail from the Cathedral Rock Picnic Area joins from the left; stay right.

0.7 The spur trail on the left leads to an unnamed spring. Stay right on the Cathedral Rock Trail.

1.3 Reach a saddle.

1.4 Reach the summit of Cathedral Rock. Return the way you came.

2.8 Arrive back at the Lower Cathedral Trailhead.

5 Griffith Peak

Griffith Peak is the 11,063-foot summit on the southeast end of the Charleston Peak ridge (known locally as the South Rim). It was named for Senator E. W. Griffith, who developed the Charleston Park resort area in Kyle Canyon. Griffith Peak is a good alternative summit for those who don't have the time to do either of the long trails to Charleston Peak.

Start: 37.5 miles northwest of Las Vegas
Distance: 8.8 miles out and back
Approximate hiking time: 7 hours
Difficulty: Strenuous due to 3,400-foot elevation change and high elevations
Trail surface: Dirt, rocks, old roads
Best seasons: Summer through fall
Water: None
Other trail users: Horses
Canine compatibility: Leashed dogs permitted
Fees and permits: None
Schedule: Open all hours
Maps: CalTopo.com MapBuilder Topo layer; USGS Charleston Peak, Griffith Peak

Trail contacts: Spring Mountains National Recreation Area, Humboldt-Toiyabe National Forest, 4701 N. Torrey Pines Dr., Las Vegas 89130-2301; (702) 872-5486; https://www .fs.usda.gov/htnf
Special considerations: This is a high-altitude hike, and some hikers may be affected by the thin air. Unlike the trails to Charleston Peak, the hike up Griffith Peak is not above timberline, so it is a good choice on windy days. Although the summit may be windy and cold, a short descent brings you back into the shelter of the forest on the west slopes of Kyle Canyon.

Finding the trailhead: From the intersection of US 95 and I-15 in downtown Las Vegas, drive 16.7 miles northwest on US 95. Turn left on NV 157, Kyle Canyon Road, and drive 20.8 miles to the Lower Cathedral Trailhead, on the right. Parking is limited, so it is best to arrive early, especially on weekends. There is additional parking in the Cathedral Rock Picnic Area just up the road. Entry to the picnic area requires a fee. GPS: N36 15.455' / W115 38.974'

The Hike

Walk up the road into the picnic area and watch for the sign marking the South Loop Trailhead. Turn right on the South Loop Trail, which climbs steadily as it crosses the hillside above the picnic area. Some portions of the lower section follow old roads, but most of the trail is a footpath. As the trail climbs below impressive Echo Cliff, it traverses a delightful mixed forest of ponderosa pine and quaking aspen.

The trail crosses the major avalanche path that descends a drainage from the north face of Griffith Peak, and skirts the base of another towering limestone cliff. The South Loop Trail crosses the drainage again and then begins switchbacking up the west side of the canyon. The ponderosa pines disappear and are replaced by white fir, bristlecone pine, and limber pine. After the trail swings around the end of a ridge, it crosses a minor drainage and avalanche path and continues to climb in well-graded

It's a different world when you stand on Griffith Peak and see the Las Vegas Strip below.

MOUNTAIN AVALANCHES

Avalanches are common in the Spring Mountains during the winter and spring months. Numerous active avalanche paths descend the south side of Kyle Canyon, and the lower portion of the South Loop Trail climbs up a major avalanche path below Griffith Peak. A forest of small quaking aspen trees covers the lower portion of the avalanche path. These trees are young and all the same height, which shows that they are regrowth following a major avalanche that swept away the previous forest. By tree ring–dating the trees, it is possible to determine the year in which the avalanche occurred.

Avalanches on a given slide path vary in size depending on snow conditions, and not all avalanches reach the bottom of the slide path. Some avalanches involve only the top layers of snow and only slide partway down the path. Others, known as "climax avalanches," involve the entire snowpack, right down to the ground. These are the slides that tend to take out large trees.

Regardless of size, all snow avalanches are dangerous. Winter hikers and mountaineers should learn about avalanches, including how to travel safely through avalanche terrain—and when not to travel through avalanche areas.

switchbacks. A sign that you are nearing the top of the switchbacks is the forest, which becomes a pure stand of bristlecone pines. The South Loop Trail finally reaches the South Rim in a saddle.

Turn left on the Griffith Peak Trail and hike toward Griffith Peak, which is clearly visible ahead. The trail crosses a saddle and meadow. Just as the trail starts up the peak itself, an unmarked hiker trail forks left from the Griffith Peak Trail. Follow this informal trail directly up the northwest ridge to the summit. It's a steep but short climb, and the views are worth the effort. Everything from the top of the Red Rock Escarpment at Red Rock Canyon to the Las Vegas Strip, the Grand Wash Cliffs at the western end of the Grand Canyon, and Kyle Canyon and the surrounding peaks is laid out before you.

The view from Griffith Peak really brings home the fact that the Spring Mountains are a cool island in a sea of desert. Plants and animals that grow and live in the Spring Mountains are isolated from similar habitat on neighboring ranges such as the Sheep Mountains by an uncrossable gulf of desert heat and aridity. Although birds can move freely between ranges, and seeds can be carried by birds or in some cases drift on the wind, these are exceptions. Since most animals and nearly all plants adapt to specific conditions, they are unable to survive a crossing of the desert valleys.

The situation was different during the glacial periods, when cooler, wetter weather probably lowered the piñon–juniper woodland to the valley floors. Then, more animals would have been able to migrate between ranges. As the climate warmed and dried after the last glacial period ended about 10,000 years ago, plants and animals migrated up the mountainsides in order to survive. Isolated from other populations,

GREEN TIP:
Borrow, rent, or share gear.

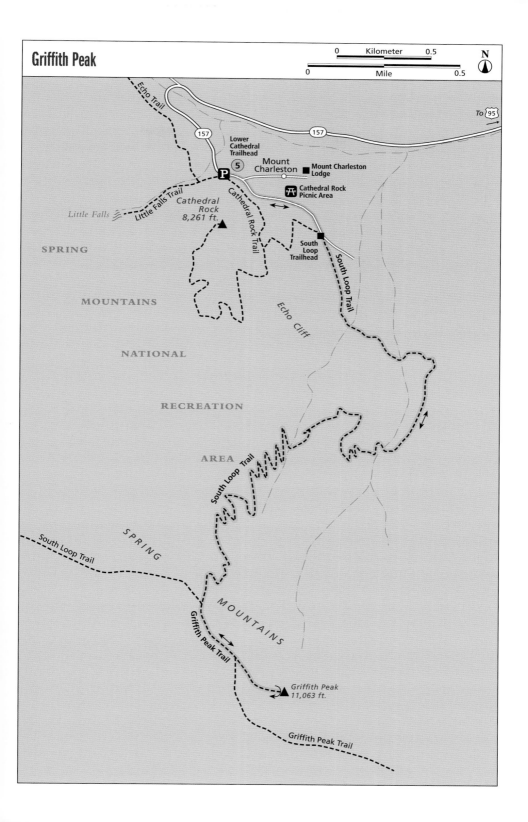

Griffith Peak

0   Kilometer   0.5

0   Mile   0.5

N

Echo Trail

To 95

157

157

Lower
Cathedral
Trailhead

5

P

Mount
Charleston

Mount Charleston
Lodge

Cathedral Rock
Picnic Area

Little Falls Trail

Little Falls

Cathedral
Rock
8,261 ft.

Cathedral Rock Trail

South
Loop
Trailhead

South Loop Trail

SPRING

MOUNTAINS

Echo Cliff

NATIONAL

RECREATION

AREA

South Loop Trail

SPRING

South Loop Trail

MOUNTAINS

Griffith Peak Trail

Griffith Peak
11,063 ft.

Griffith Peak Trail

these plants and animals tended to evolve in different directions, which is why mountains such as the Spring Mountains are home to species that are found nowhere else on earth.

Miles and Directions

0.0 From the Lower Cathedral Trailhead, walk up the road into the Cathedral Rock Picnic Area.

0.4 From the South Loop Trailhead, start on the South Loop Trail.

1.0 The South Loop Trail crosses the drainage in the avalanche path below Griffith Peak.

1.5 The trail crosses the drainage again and climbs the west slopes of the canyon.

2.0 Cross the ridge and follow the trail southwest across a minor avalanche path.

4.0 Arrive at the junction with the Griffith Peak Trail in a saddle on the South Rim. Turn left on the Griffith Peak Trail.

4.1 The Griffith Peak Trail crosses a meadow in a saddle. Griffith Peak is visible just ahead.

4.2 Leave the Griffith Peak Trail and turn left on an unsigned hiker trail. Follow this informal trail directly up the northwest ridge of Griffith Peak.

4.4 Reach Griffith Peak. Return the way you came.

8.8 Arrive back at the Lower Cathedral Trailhead.

6 Charleston Peak via South Loop Trail

Charleston Peak, at 11,811 feet, is the highest point in the Spring Mountains as well as southern Nevada. There are two main trails to the summit: South Loop Trail and Trail Canyon–North Loop. Both offer about the same length and difficulty, but the scenery and the final approach to the summit are different. This approach, via the South Loop Trail, gets nearly all the climbing over early and then traverses the long, scenic South Rim ridge from Griffith Peak to Charleston Peak, passing through one of the most extensive bristlecone forests in Nevada.

Start: 37.5 miles northwest of Las Vegas
Distance: 16.4 miles out and back
Approximate hiking time: 10 hours
Difficulty: Strenuous due to 4,270-foot elevation change and high elevations
Trail surface: Dirt and rocks, short sections of old road near the start
Best seasons: Summer through fall
Water: None
Other trail users: Horses
Canine compatibility: Leashed dogs permitted
Fees and permits: None
Schedule: Open all hours
Maps: CalTopo.com MapBuilder Topo layer; USGS Charleston Peak, Griffith Peak

Trail contacts: Spring Mountains National Recreation Area, Humboldt-Toiyabe National Forest, 4701 N. Torrey Pines Dr., Las Vegas 89130-2301; (702) 872-5486; https://www.fs.usda.gov/htnf

Special considerations: Be aware that this is a high-altitude hike and that a portion is above timberline, where there is no protection from high wind. Bring windproof outer clothing, a warm pullover cap, and gloves, and be prepared for changing weather. If thunderstorms are threatening, get off the exposed ridge and the peak as quickly as possible.

Finding the trailhead: From the intersection of US 95 and I-15 in downtown Las Vegas, drive 16.7 miles northwest on US 95. Turn left on NV 157, Kyle Canyon Road, and drive 20.8 miles to the Lower Cathedral Trailhead, on the right. Parking is limited, so it is best to arrive early, especially on weekends. There is additional parking in the Cathedral Rock Picnic Area just up the road. Entry to the picnic area requires a fee. GPS: N36 15.455' / W115 38.974'

The Hike

From the trailhead the South Loop Trail climbs above the picnic area, traversing through a mixed forest of mountain mahogany, ponderosa pine, and quaking aspen. Climbing steadily, the trail crosses the canyon above the picnic area, and then climbs steeply along the east side of the canyon, following an old road. The old road ends and the trail narrows where it crosses the canyon again, below towering limestone cliffs. The canyon is clearly a major avalanche path, as shown by the destroyed trees and small aspens growing in the canyon bottom.

Switchbacks lead up the north side of the canyon until the trail is above the cliffs. The South Loop Trail then climbs out of the canyon to the north and switchbacks up a broad ridge. The first limber and bristlecone pines appear at this point. A couple of the switchbacks provide views overlooking Charleston Peak miles to the north. The trail continues its well-graded but steady climb to the ridge south of Charleston Peak, known locally as the South Rim. A sign that you're nearing the South Rim is the disappearance of all trees except for bristlecone pines.

At the ridge a sign marks the junction with the Griffith Peak Trail, coming in from the left. Stay right on the South Loop Trail, and follow it north toward Charleston Peak. The trail skirts the edge of the South Rim and traverses beautiful alpine meadows and groves of bristlecone pines. Occasionally the trail passes through a saddle on the rim and lets you look down into Kyle Canyon, now more than 3,000 feet below.

As the trail gradually climbs, it begins skirting the edge of timberline as it traverses the western slopes of the South Rim. After the last trees are left behind, the trail begins the final ascent of the mountain. Watch for an unmarked spur trail on the right above a saddle, which leads to the scattered wreckage of a plane that crashed here in 1955.

Above the crash site the South Loop Trail swings around to the west and climbs to the summit of Charleston Peak via a final switchback up the western slopes. The windswept summit is marked by a couple of solar-powered radio repeaters, an aluminum benchmark disk, and a summit register mounted on a short pole. A rock shelter just to the north offers some protection from the wind.

▶ Notice how the bristlecones growing just below the South Rim are relatively tall and slender, at least for bristlecone pines, and the trees growing along the South Rim and its western slopes are short and squat. That's because the trees on the east slopes are more protected from prevailing winter storms, which come out of the west. The trees along the South Rim ridge must endure much harsher winter weather, but as a result they live much longer than the more sheltered trees.

Charleston Peak was named for the city of Charleston, South Carolina, by a topographic mapping group of the US Army Corps of Engineers in 1869. The native Southern Paiutes called the peak *Nuvant,* and it was the most famous place in the mythology of the Chemehuevi and the western bands of the Southern Paiute.

This hike showcases how life adapts to increasing elevation and harsher conditions. During the ascent from the trailhead to the South Rim and the junction with the Griffith Peak Trail, you are climbing through a forest that is protected from the prevailing southwest winds by the slope's northeast aspect. As a result the trees grow tall and slender as they compete with their fellow trees for sunlight. This tendency is especially apparent in the ponderosa pines that grow on the lower slopes just above the trailhead. Mature ponderosa pines drop their lower branches so that the bottom 20 or 30 feet of the trunk is bare of limbs. Ponderosa pines are very heat-tolerant as long as they get enough water, so they are typically the lowest tall trees growing in the Nevada mountain ranges. Cold limits their upper range, so as you climb you'll see more cold-tolerant trees such as limber pine, Douglas fir, and white fir mixing in with the ponderosa pines, and finally replacing them.

One adaptation that evergreen trees make to cold is to grow denser foliage, which conserves heat. Limber pines have needles in tight bunches of five, as opposed to the looser bundles of three on ponderosa pines. This effect is even more pronounced in Engelmann spruce, whose single short needles are crowded together on the branches. Likewise, bristlecone pines, which you'll encounter as you near the top of the climb to the South Rim, have five short needles tightly bunched together.

Another adaptation to cold is huddling. As you continue northwest along the ridge toward Charleston Peak and approach timberline, you'll notice that the trees are shorter and tend to grow in small groves. By growing together in such clusters, trees give each other protection from the fiercely cold winter winds and blowing snow.

Krummholz is another adaptation and is common right at timberline. Because the icy

The dense, resinous wood of bristlecone pines resists decay long after the tree has died. Researchers can tree ring–date bristlecone snags and logs, correlate their growth rings with living trees, and extend the tree ring record thousands of years further into the past. That's one of the reasons campfires are not allowed in any of the three wilderness areas in the Spring Mountains.

wind and abrasive blowing snow tend to kill exposed tree limbs and needles, the only surviving trees are small and grow in dense mats behind a boulder or a rock ledge. The obstruction tends to protect the foliage from wind and driven snow as well as causing snowdrifts to form on their lee sides, providing further protection. Some krummholz appear to have no protection, but they are protected by snowdrifts that regularly form in the same place because of variations in the terrain.

When a tree does manage to send up a vertical trunk above the protective mat, the wind kills all the branches on the upwind side, so the remaining branches appear to be streaming downwind like a flag, which is why these trees are often referred to as "flag trees."

On the final climb of Charleston Peak, beyond the crash site, the only plants that can survive the arctic conditions grow low to the ground, often in mats. Seasonal wildflowers must flower and go to seed quickly in order to reproduce before the short growing season comes to an end.

Charleston Peak via South Loop Trail

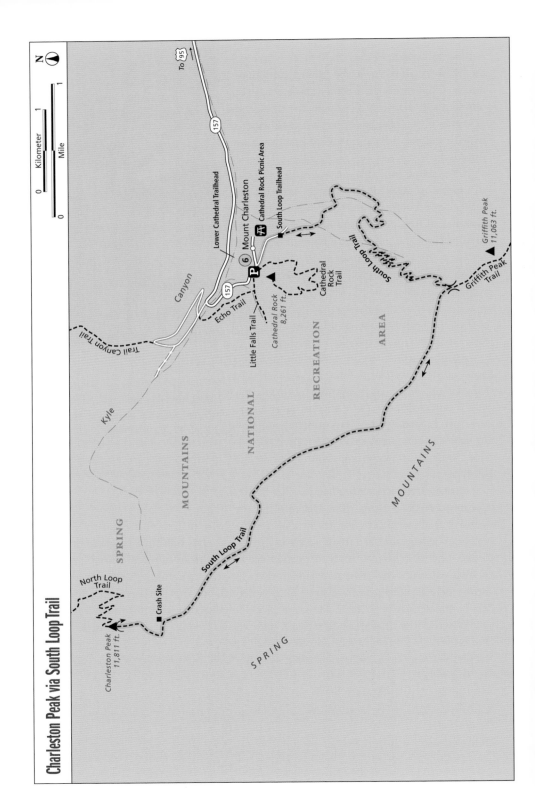

PLANE CRASH SITE

On November 17, 1955, an Air Force C-54 transport plane crashed into the slopes of Charleston Peak just south of the summit, apparently during bad weather. The crash, the aircraft mission, and even the names of the fourteen men who died in the crash were kept secret until 2001. The plane was flying from Palmdale, California, to Groom Lake, the top-secret military test center north of Las Vegas. Aboard were some of the designers and engineers involved in the highly classified U2 spy plane, as well as the flight crew. Apparently the pilot was flying in and out of clouds and misjudged a turn, striking the mountain at the 11,400-foot level. Over the years much of the wreckage has been carried off by souvenir hunters.

The tangled wreckage of a miltary transport plane that crashed in 1955 lies just south of Charleston Peak.

Miles and Directions

0.0   From the Lower Cathedral Trailhead, walk up the road into the Cathedral Rock Picnic Area.

0.4   From the South Loop Trailhead, start on the South Loop Trail.

1.0   The South Loop Trail crosses the drainage in the avalanche path below Griffith Peak.

1.5   The trail crosses the drainage again and climbs the west slopes of the canyon.

2.0   Cross the ridge and follow the trail southwest across a minor avalanche path.

4.0   Reach a junction with the Griffith Peak Trail in a saddle on the South Rim. Stay right on the South Loop Trail.

7.7   An unmarked hiker trail turns right and leads to the wreckage from a 1955 plane crash.

7.8   Rejoin the South Loop Trail; stay right.

8.2   Reach Charleston Peak. Return the way you came.

16.4   Arrive back at Lower Cathedral Trailhead.

7 Mummy Spring via Trail Canyon

The striking cliffs of 11,296-foot Mummy Mountain are a major landmark along the high ridges of the Spring Mountains, and are visible for miles. The mountain gets its name from the obvious resemblance to an Egyptian mummy, especially when viewed from east or west. This hike takes you up Trail Canyon past the oldest known bristlecone pine in the range, and ends at a spring nestled below towering limestone cliffs.

Start: 37.6 miles northwest of Las Vegas
Distance: 7.6 miles out and back
Approximate hiking time: 7 hours
Difficulty: Strenuous due to 2,100-foot elevation change
Trail surface: Dirt, rocks, old roads
Best seasons: Spring through fall
Water: Mummy Spring
Other trail users: Horses
Canine compatibility: Leashed dogs permitted

Fees and permits: None
Schedule: Open all hours
Maps: CalTopo.com MapBuilder Topo layer; USGS Charleston Peak
Trail contacts: Spring Mountains National Recreation Area, Humboldt-Toiyabe National Forest, 4701 N. Torrey Pines Dr., Las Vegas 89130-2301; (702) 872-5486; https://www.fs.usda.gov/htnf

Finding the trailhead: From the intersection of US 95 and I-15 in downtown Las Vegas, drive 16.7 miles northwest on US 95. Turn left on NV 157, Kyle Canyon Road, and drive 20.0 miles. Bear right onto Echo Road and continue 0.9 mile to the Trail Canyon Trailhead. GPS: N36 16.050'/W115 39.482'

The Hike

The start of the hike on the Trail Canyon Trail follows a service road to a waterstorage tank. Beyond the tank the trail follows a closed jeep trail directly up Trail Canyon, and the climb is relentless. In compensation you're walking up through a fine mixed forest of quaking aspen, mountain mahogany, and ponderosa pine.

Near the head of the canyon, the trail becomes a foot trail, the grade eases somewhat, and the trail veers out of the canyon on the right. Switchbacks lead to a saddle and the junction with the North Loop Trail. Turn right on the North Loop Trail and continue northeast under the imposing cliffs of Mummy Mountain. The North Loop Trail climbs at a moderate rate and finally reaches another saddle, this one located directly east of the east end of Mummy Mountain.

GREEN TIP:
Reuse ziplock plastic bags by turning them inside out and washing them in your washing machine along with your clothes.

In the saddle a huge bristlecone pine, dubbed the Rain Tree, has been estimated to be more than 3,000 years old, which would make it the oldest bristlecone pine in the Spring Range. Bristlecone pines (and other trees) can be dated by taking non-destructive core samples, but this has apparently not been done with Rain Tree.

Leave the saddle by turning left onto a distinct but unmarked trail. This trail descends gradually to end at Mummy Spring, which drips over a limestone ledge. The gully containing the spring is also an avalanche path, judging by the aspen reproduction below the spring. The open ravine below the spring also gives you a view out to the north, toward the Sheep Range.

Insects and bees are commonly seen around springs and other isolated water sources. While most stinging insects such as wasps and bees will leave you alone if you don't molest them, there is one notable exception: Africanized honeybees. Popularly known as "killer bees," Africanized honeybees appear identical to the common European honeybee, but are significantly more aggressive. An exotic or non-native species, they were accidentally introduced into the wild in South America about 1970 and have since spread into the United States.

Africanized honeybees are more easily disturbed than European honeybees, are more likely to attack, attack in greater numbers, and are more persistent. Like their calmer counterparts, Africanized honeybees can nest anywhere there is a suitable spot for a hive—in the walls of buildings, utility meter boxes, and in abandoned cars and other junk. In the wild they nest in caves or hollows, in animal burrows, among rocks, and in trees. Encounters in the wild are rare—nearly all attacks are in urban or suburban areas.

The sting of the Africanized honeybee is no more potent than that of the European honeybee, but animals and people attacked by Africanized bees typically

Rain Tree, which grows in the saddle at the junction of the North Loop Trail and the spur trail to Mummy Spring, is regarded as the oldest bristlecone pine in the Spring Mountains, at over 3,000 years.

▶ **The Sheep Range, visible in the distance from Mummy Spring, is part of the Desert National Wildlife Refuge, which was established to protect the native desert bighorn sheep. Bighorns require large amounts of remote land for their survival, and the seldom-visited Sheep Range, although visible from the heavily populated Las Vegas area, is ideal habitat.**

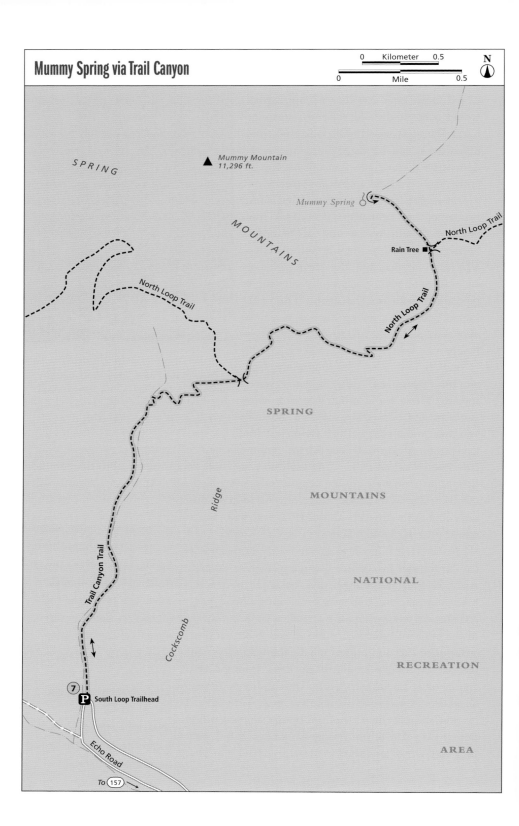

Mummy Spring via Trail Canyon

0   Kilometer   0.5

0   Mile   0.5

N

SPRING

▲ Mummy Mountain
11,296 ft.

MOUNTAINS

Mummy Spring

North Loop Trail

Rain Tree

North Loop Trail

North Loop Trail

SPRING

Ridge

MOUNTAINS

NATIONAL

Trail Canyon Trail

Cockscomb

RECREATION

7 P South Loop Trailhead

AREA

Echo Road

To 157

DENDROCHRONOLOGY, THE ART OF DATING TREES

Trees can be dated precisely by taking core samples with a tree-boring tool, which does not harm the tree. The core samples are studied in a lab, where the number of annual growth rings is counted. Each ring corresponds to one year in the life of the tree. Much additional information can be learned from the core samples, including how dry or wet the climate was during the tree's life. Since dead trees and downed bristlecone logs decay very slowly, tree ring samples from dead wood can be correlated to living trees to extend the climate record even further back in time, currently more than 9,000 years.

suffer hundreds or even thousands of stings, often with a fatal result. Of course, if you have an allergy to bee stings, then even a single sting is dangerous. Africanized bees appear to be especially sensitive to loud vibrations and to odors, and tend to attack furry and dark-colored objects.

When hiking, avoid all bees and especially any that are swarming. Avoid anything that is scented, including scented soap, shampoo, hair spray, perfumes and colognes, and chewing gum. If you're hiking with a dog, keep it on a leash and do not let it roam through brush. Dogs have triggered a number of attacks.

If attacked, seek the shelter of a vehicle or building if available. In the backcountry run and keep running. Africanized bees commonly pursue for 0.25 to 0.5 mile. Don't fight or flail at the bees—the scent of crushed bees further incites their attack. Africanized bees go for your head and face, so cover your head with loose clothing and protect your face. Run through brush or dense foliage if it is handy—dense vegetation confuses bees.

Miles and Directions

0.0 Start on the Trail Canyon Trail.

0.8 At the end of an old road, the climb moderates somewhat.

1.9 At the saddle and junction with the North Loop Trail, turn right onto North Loop Trail.

3.4 At the saddle and Rain Tree, turn left on the unmarked trail to Mummy Spring.

3.8 Arrive at Mummy Spring, which is located in an avalanche path. Return the way you came.

7.6 Arrive back at the Trail Canyon Trailhead.

8 Charleston Peak via Trail Canyon

This is the other approach to Charleston Peak, using the Trail Canyon and North Loop Trails. (You can also start from the North Loop Trailhead, but the hike from Trail Canyon Trailhead is shorter.) Like the South Loop Trail, this approach gets most of the climbing out of the way early, but the scenery and aspect of the final approach along the North Rim (the local name for the head of Kyle Canyon) is quite different. The hike is slightly shorter and there is a bit less elevation gain, but the two routes are both very long day hikes.

Start: 37.6 miles northwest of Las Vegas
Distance: 15.8 miles out and back
Approximate hiking time: 8–9 hours
Difficulty: Strenuous due to 4,070-foot elevation change and high elevations
Trail surface: Dirt and rocks, old roads
Best seasons: Summer and fall
Water: Cave Spring
Other trail users: Horses
Canine compatibility: Leashed dogs permitted
Fees and permits: None
Schedule: Open all hours
Maps: CalTopo.com MapBuilder Topo layer; USGS Charleston Peak

Trail contacts: Spring Mountains National Recreation Area, Humboldt-Toiyabe National Forest, 4701 N. Torrey Pines Dr., Las Vegas 89130-2301; (702) 872-5486; https://www.fs.usda.gov/htnf
Special considerations: Be aware that this is a high-altitude hike and that a portion is above timberline where there is no protection from high wind. Bring windproof outer clothing, a warm pullover cap, and gloves, and be prepared for changing weather. If thunderstorms are threatening, get off the exposed peak as quickly as possible.

Finding the trailhead: From the intersection of US 95 and I-15 in downtown Las Vegas, drive 16.7 miles northwest on US 95. Turn left on NV 157, Kyle Canyon Road, and drive 20 miles. Bear right onto Echo Road and continue 0.9 mile to the Trail Canyon Trailhead. GPS: N36 16.050' / W115 39.482'

The Hike

The start of the hike on the Trail Canyon Trail follows a service road to a water-storage tank. Beyond the tank the trail follows a closed jeep trail directly up Trail Canyon, and the climb is relentless but beautiful—you're climbing through a fine mixed forest of quaking aspen, mountain mahogany, and ponderosa pine.

Near the head of the canyon, the trail becomes a foot trail, the grade eases somewhat, and the trail veers out of the canyon on the right. Switchbacks lead to a saddle

GREEN TIP:
Donate used gear to a nonprofit organization for kids.

CLIMATE CHANGE

Dead wood from bristlecone pines can be found above the current level of timberline. The presence of this wood indicates that bristlecone pines used to grow higher up the mountain slopes than they do at present. In the White Mountains of California, bristlecones once grew about 500 feet higher than they do now, which indicates that the climate was somewhat warmer in the recent past. The presence of seedlings growing above the mature trees indicates that the climate is again warming.

and the junction with the North Loop Trail. Turn left on the North Loop Trail to continue toward Charleston Peak, which is visible through the trees to the southwest.

Above the saddle the North Loop Trail heads generally west, climbing the slopes below Mummy Mountain at a steady gradient. You'll soon come out onto a slope that was burned in an old forest fire. Small aspen trees are starting the reforestation process. In late September the aspen turn bright yellow and orange, splashing the mountainside with color. An old watering trough cut from a single log marks Cave Spring. After the spring the trail turns sharply right in a single long switchback, which crosses the top of the old burn area to the base of the cliffs below Mummy Mountain. Turning left at the end of the switchback, the North Loop Trail now heads back toward Charleston Peak, climbing steadily toward the ridge between Mummy Mountain and Charleston Peak.

Eventually the trail reaches the actual North Rim, and for the first time you get a view to the north, over the head of Lee Canyon and toward the northernmost summits in the Spring Range. At this point you've climbed more than 3,000 feet and have less than 1,000 to go to reach the summit. On the other hand, if it's past noon, especially in the fall when the days are short, you may want to consider turning

The long approach to Charleston Peak on the North Loop Trail passes through miles of ancient bristlecone pines.

Several solar-powered radio repeaters and a summit register mounted on a pole mark the rounded summit of Charleston Peak.

▶ **As you approach timberline, stop in the shelter of the last of the trees and layer on more clothing to protect you from the cold wind that is usually present on exposed alpine summits. If that would cause you to overheat, at least keep the layers at the top of your pack where they are easy to reach. And make certain that a warm hat and your gloves are handy. If you can hear the wind blowing above you, put on your wind shell. It's a lot easier to do in a calm, sheltered spot than on a wind-whipped summit.**

back. The descent from Charleston Peak will take at least four hours for most hikers.

If you elect to continue, you'll be following the North Loop Trail along the North Rim as it skirts minor summits on the left, above Kyle Canyon, and passes through several saddles. A final saddle features a small rock pinnacle, the Devils Thumb, and marks the start of the final ascent of Charleston Peak. The North Loop Trail heads across the east face of the mountain, picking its way across narrow ledges between lime-stone cliff bands. Tenacious bristlecone pines cling to the ledges, proving that these hardy trees do best in exposed, severe locations near timberline.

After clearing the last of the ledges, the trail switchbacks up a broad talus slope to the summit. The summit itself is a rounded north–south ridge, and the high point is marked by an aluminum benchmark disk and a summit register mounted on a short pole. When you've had your fill of the views, retrace your steps to the trailhead.

MOUNTAINTOP RADIO SITES

Several solar-powered electronic sites huddle on the wind-blasted summit of Charleston Peak. The reason these units are present is because agencies such as the USDA Forest Service communicate in the field using very high frequency (VHF) or ultra high frequency (UHF) radios. Amateur radio operators (hams) also use VHF and UHF frequencies to communicate. While VHF and UHF radio have many advantages, such as freedom from interference, lack of fading from sunspots and other solar activity, and reliable communications in any weather, one disadvantage is that these frequencies are line-of-sight, just like light waves. That means that a forest worker using a mobile or handheld radio in a place such as Kyle Canyon would not be able to reach a station in Lee Canyon or Las Vegas, for example.

Common solutions to this problem are to set up radio repeaters or remote bases on high points and mountaintops. A radio repeater receives a transmission on one frequency and simultaneously retransmits it on another frequency. As long as the two stations that wish to communicate can see the mountaintop repeater, they can talk to each other. Radio repeaters placed on high points such as Charleston Peak can greatly increase the range and usefulness of portable and mobile two-way radio.

Sometimes a remote base station is set up on a mountaintop, usually to facilitate communications with a base station or dispatch office located in a central location, such as Las Vegas. In this case the dispatch office communicates with the remote base through a dedicated radio link, and the remote base repeats this transmission to field stations. The field stations can use the remote base to talk to the dispatch office, but not to each other.

Since many mountaintop radio sites are not connected to the electric power grid, they must generate their own power on-site. Even sites with commercial power often have their own power sources for backup. The most common power source is solar electric panels because they are durable and require little maintenance. Since the panels produce power only when the sun is shining, the radio site must have enough battery storage to keep the site running during the night and through periods of cloudy weather. This is especially critical during the winter when the days are short.

Other power sources that are used at remote sites include diesel or gas generators and wind turbines. Wind is difficult to use on a high mountain peak because of ice accumulations. During winter storms when the summit is in the clouds and high winds are present, supercooled water droplets (droplets that remain liquid below the freezing point) instantly freeze on contact with solid objects. Such rime ice can build up to more than a foot thick, enough to unbalance and destroy a wind turbine or, at best, turn the blades into a nonrotating blob of ice.

Charleston Peak via Trail Canyon

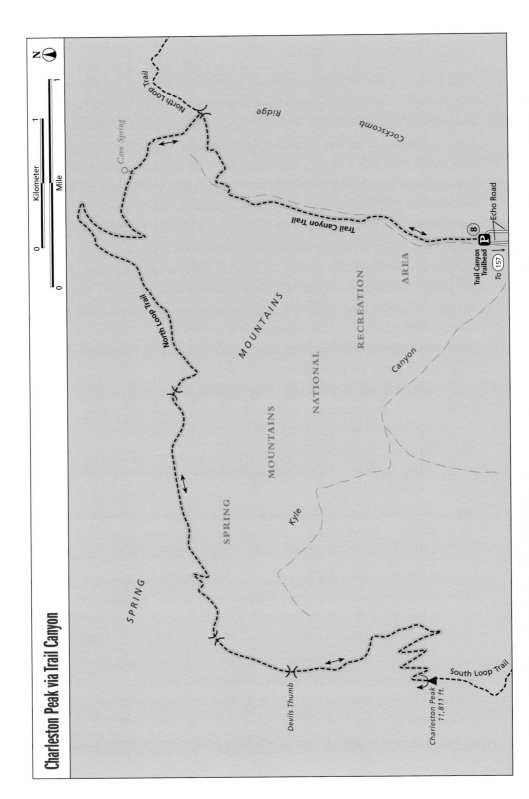

N

Kilometer
0   1

Mile
0   1

North Loop Trail

Cave Spring

Cockscomb Ridge

North Loop Trail

Trail Canyon Trail

Echo Road

8

P

Trail Canyon Trailhead

To 157

Kyle Canyon

SPRING MOUNTAINS NATIONAL RECREATION AREA

SPRING MOUNTAINS

Devils Thumb

Charleston Peak 11,811 ft.

South Loop Trail

Miles and Directions

0.0 Start up the Trail Canyon Trail from the Trail Canyon Trailhead.

0.8 At the end of an old road, the climb moderates somewhat.

1.9 At the saddle and junction with North Loop Trail, turn left onto North Loop Trail.

2.4 Arrive at Cave Spring and continue on the North Loop Trail.

4.1 The North Loop Trail reaches the North Rim and levels out.

6.3 The saddle at Devils Thumb is the last saddle before starting the final ascent of Charleston Peak.

7.1 Reach the end of the traverse along the ledges on the east face of Charleston Peak. The trail now starts climbing via switchbacks.

7.9 Reach Charleston Peak. Return the way you came.

15.8 Arrive back at the Trail Canyon Trailhead.

GREEN TIP:

Pass it down—the best way to instill good green habits in your children is to set a good example.

9 Mary Jane Falls

Probably the most popular hike in the Spring Mountains, the reputation of this well-graded trail is deserved. The hike takes you through fine alpine forest into the cliff-bound head of Kyle Canyon and ends at a permanent waterfall.

Start: 37.6 miles northwest of Las Vegas
Distance: 3.0 miles out and back
Approximate hiking time: 2–3 hours
Difficulty: Moderate due to 1,100-foot elevation change
Trail surface: Dirt and rocks
Best seasons: Spring through fall
Water: Mary Jane Falls
Other trail users: Horses
Canine compatibility: Leashed dogs permitted

Fees and permits: None
Schedule: Open all hours
Maps: CalTopo.com MapBuilder Topo layer; USGS Charleston Peak
Trail contacts: Spring Mountains National Recreation Area, Humboldt-Toiyabe National Forest, 4701 N. Torrey Pines Dr., Las Vegas 89130-2301; (702) 872-5486; https://www.fs.usda.gov/htnf

Finding the trailhead: From the intersection of US 95 and I-15 in downtown Las Vegas, drive 16.7 miles northwest on US 95. Turn left on NV 157, Kyle Canyon Road, and drive 20.5 miles. Bear right onto Echo Road and continue 0.4 mile. Turn left at the Mary Jane Falls turnoff and drive 0.2 mile to the Mary Jane Falls Trailhead. GPS: N36 16.044' / W115 39.756'

The Hike

From the trailhead the Mary Jane Falls Trail climbs west up the north side of the broad head of Kyle Canyon, climbing steadily but not too steeply through beautiful stands of quaking aspen, ponderosa pine, white fir, and Douglas fir. Watch for the point where the trail abruptly switchbacks to the right and leaves the canyon bottom. A series of well-graded switchbacks ascend to the north, finally leading to the base of an imposing limestone cliff. The trail then turns northwest and follows the base of the cliff to Mary Jane Falls. The falls are best in the spring after a snowy winter, but they run all year long. On a hot day it's pleasant to climb into the large cave at the base of the falls and cool off, but use care negotiating the mossy, slippery rocks. A short trail leads left from the falls to a small cave.

Rattlesnakes are present throughout North America into southern Canada from sea level to near timberline and are found as high as 10,000 feet right here in the Spring Mountains. In reality the tiny desert bark scorpion is far more dangerous, having killed ten times as many people as rattlesnakes in Arizona—a state with a lot of rattlesnakes. Rattlesnakes present a manageable hazard on the trail, and you are more likely to be injured on the way to the trailhead by a driver yakking on a cell phone than you are by a rattlesnake.

The rattlesnake's unique rattle is defensive and serves to warn away large animals. Since rattlesnakes used to share habitats with large hoofed animals such as bison and elk, and still coexist with domestic cattle, the shrill, unmistakable sound of the rattle is a great defense. The rattle itself consists of hollow buttons, or

▶ **Mary Jane Falls flows all year but is most spectacular in the spring after a snowy winter.**

segments, of kerotin (the same protein-based material that forms hair and fingernails), which grow on the tail. Although mature rattlesnakes usually give hikers plenty of warning by shaking their tails so fast that they are a blur, they don't always rattle—most snakes sense you before you're even aware of their presence and move quietly away. Young rattlesnakes have a single button, and although they may shake their tail furiously, they don't produce a sound. They do have venom, though.

A member of the pit viper family, rattlesnakes hunt mice and other small rodents and mammals by sensing ground vibrations, by smell, and by infrared light. The "pits" that give pit vipers their name are actually organs sensitive to infrared light, which humans cannot see. Because infrared light is given off by warm objects, warm-blooded mammals stand out against their backgrounds when viewed in infrared.

When the rattlesnake strikes its prey, it injects toxic venom through a pair of fangs that are hollow like a hypodermic needle. The fangs fold back against the roof of the snake's mouth when not in use. Rattlesnake venom is hemotoxic, or tissue-destructive. The venom has two functions: first, to immediately paralyze the snake's prey so it can't run off, and second, to start the digestive process. Rattlesnakes swallow their prey whole, so they can't handle prey that can run away or fight back.

Most human victims of rattlesnakes are snake collectors or people attempting to handle or tease rattlesnakes. And more bites take place around human habitation than in the wild. For the hiker, a little bit of knowledge can reduce the rattlesnake hazard to almost zero.

Contrary to the popular notion that rattlesnakes thrive in scorching heat, they are cold-blooded like all reptiles and take their body temperature from their environment. Since they prefer a body temperature of about 80 degrees Fahrenheit, they prefer

Mature ponderosa pines have thick, orange-colored bark that is thick and platy, which helps protect the tree against wildfires. This tree has been struck by lightning.

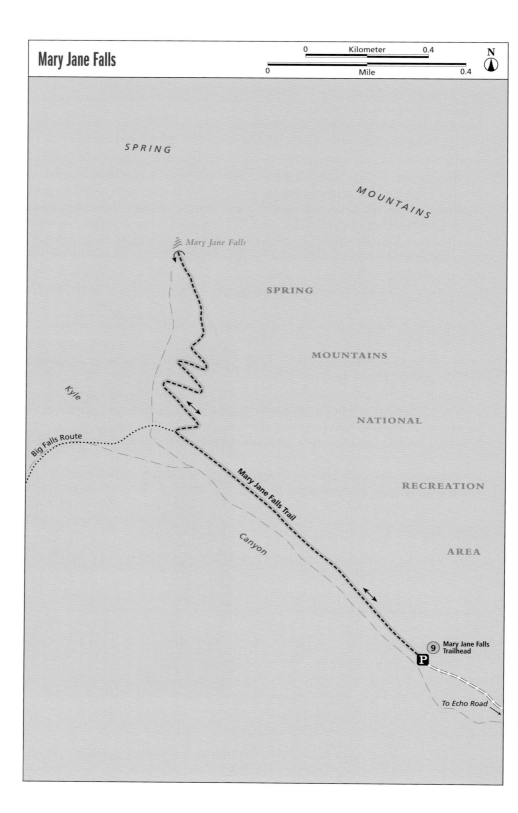

Mary Jane Falls

SPRING

MOUNTAINS

SPRING

MOUNTAINS

NATIONAL

RECREATION

AREA

Mary Jane Falls

Kyle

Big Falls Route

Mary Jane Falls Trail

Canyon

9 Mary Jane Falls Trailhead

P

To Echo Road

Kilometer
0   0.4

Mile
0   0.4

N

CAVE FORMATION

Caves such as the ones at Mary Jane Falls are common in limestone formations such as those in the Spring Mountains. The major component of limestone rock is calcium carbonate, which dissolves in water, especially if the water is slightly acidic. Groundwater percolating through the rock naturally concentrates along cracks and other weaknesses in the rock. Eventually groundwater action can carve out huge caves, and some of these become exposed at the surface due to erosion of the landscape. Water dripping from the roof of caves and flowing across rock surfaces evaporates, leaving behind the minerals that were dissolved in the water and creating intricate rock formations.

soil or stone surfaces at about that temperature. Temperatures of 100 degrees Fahrenheit will quickly kill a rattlesnake. When the weather is hot, rattlesnakes seek the coolness of burrows or the shade of bushes and rocks. During chilly weather, they'll emerge and sun themselves on rocks or bare dirt. And during the winter and prolonged cold spells, they'll hibernate in burrows. Rattlesnakes can only strike about half their length, although they can strike from any position, not just a defensive coil. The western diamondback, the most common rattlesnake species in Nevada, averages about 4 to 5 feet and occasionally reaches 7 feet in length. Another common rattlesnake, the Mohave, is usually smaller, but its venom is more potent.

To avoid surprises, always watch the ground ahead of you as you walk. If you want to look at distant scenery, stop first. Avoid placing your hands or feet closer than 3 feet to any place you cannot see into, such as the underside of dense brush. Don't walk close to shady overhanging rocks or ledges. Look over logs before stepping over them, or better yet, go around. If camping in warm weather, when snakes are nocturnal due to the daytime heat, sleep in a closed tent.

If someone is bitten, keep the victim calm and seek medical attention as soon as possible. Many defensive bites are dry because the snake doesn't waste venom on animals that are too large to eat. The main danger from rattlesnake bites is infection from the deep puncture wounds. Even if venom is injected, modern medical treatment uses antivenin injections that neutralize the venom and minimize tissue damage.

Miles and Directions

0.0 From the Mary Jane Falls Trailhead, follow the Mary Jane Falls Trail northwest up the canyon.

0.7 The trail turns sharply right as the unsigned route to Big Falls continues straight ahead. After you bend to the north, follow the switchbacks up the northeast slopes of the canyon below Mary Jane Falls.

1.5 Arrive at Mary Jane Falls. Return the way you came.

3.0 Arrive back at the Mary Jane Falls Trailhead.

10 Big Falls

Big Falls, as the name implies, is the highest waterfall in Kyle Canyon. It's a little harder to reach than Mary Jane Falls, and the flow is seasonal. The best time to see a dramatic waterfall is late in the spring, in April or May, when the approach is free of snow but the snowpack on the upper slopes is still melting.

Start: 37.6 miles northwest of Las Vegas
Distance: 2.8 miles out and back
Approximate hiking time: 2 hours
Difficulty: Moderate due to 900-foot elevation change
Trail surface: Dirt and rocks, cross-country, rock scrambling
Best seasons: Spring through fall
Water: Seasonal at Big Falls
Other trail users: None

Canine compatibility: Leashed dogs permitted
Fees and permits: None
Schedule: Open all hours
Maps: CalTopo.com MapBuilder Topo layer; USGS Charleston Peak
Trail contacts: Spring Mountains National Recreation Area, Humboldt-Toiyabe National Forest, 4701 N. Torrey Pines Dr., Las Vegas 89130-2301; (702) 872-5486; https://www.fs.usda.gov/htnf

Finding the trailhead: From the intersection of US 95 and I-15 in downtown Las Vegas, drive 16.7 miles northwest on US 95. Turn left on NV 157, Kyle Canyon Road, and drive 20.5 miles. Bear right onto Echo Road and continue 0.4 mile. Turn left at the Mary Jane Falls turnoff and drive 0.2 mile to the Mary Jane Falls Trailhead. GPS: N36 16.044' / W115 39.756'

The Hike

Follow the Mary Jane Falls Trail up the right side of Kyle Canyon to the point where the Mary Jane Falls Trail abruptly turns right and starts switchbacking up the north side of the canyon. Turn left here on an unofficial trail that continues to climb up the bed of Kyle Canyon. Marked by a few rock cairns, the trail gradually works its way to the left side of Kyle Canyon, and then turns left up the unnamed drainage below Big Falls. This crossing is marked by the yellow signs of a Soil Conservation Service Snow Course at the top of the bank to the left.

The route now follows the drainage directly south toward Big Falls. If the bed is dry, as is normally the case in the fall, boulder-hop directly up the bed. If the creek is running, it may be easier to follow informal trails on the west bank. As the limestone cliffs start to close in the canyon narrows, you'll come to a chockstone blocking the bed. Bypass this obstacle via a trail on the left, then continue up the bed above. Avalanche debris tends to choke the bed, and it may be easier to climb along the slopes to the right. A final bend of the canyon to the left reveals the falls, a mere damp streak in the fall but an impressive falls in the spring when the snow is melting off the slopes of Charleston Peak high above.

ROCK CLIMBING

Contrary to popular impressions, rock climbers don't normally use their ropes and equipment to help them ascend. Instead they use the rope and various types of rock anchors to safeguard themselves from a fall. The sport of rock climbing consists of working out ever-harder routes up steep and even overhanging cliffs, like those at Robbers Roost, by using natural cracks and holds to climb.

0.3 Arrive at the caves in the head of a narrow canyon. To return to the trailhead, take the trail left, out of the canyon and across the slope.

0.4 The loop ends at an unsigned trail junction, the main trail you started on. Turn right to return to the trailhead.

0.6 Cross the highway to the Robbers Roost Trailhead.

12 Fletcher Peak

A far easier summit to reach than the 11,000-foot peaks in the Spring Mountains, rounded 10,233-foot Fletcher Peak nevertheless features sweeping views, especially of Kyle Canyon and the high peaks. You'll also hike through some outstanding bristlecone pine forest.

Start: 39.1 miles northwest of Las Vegas
Distance: 5.6 miles out and back
Approximate hiking time: 4 hours
Difficulty: Strenuous due to 1,860-foot elevation change and high elevations
Trail surface: Dirt and rocks
Best seasons: Spring through fall
Water: None
Other trail users: Horses
Canine compatibility: Leashed dogs permitted

Fees and permits: None
Schedule: Open all hours
Maps: CalTopo.com MapBuilder Topo layer; USGS Angel Peak, Charleston Peak
Trail contacts: Spring Mountains National Recreation Area, Humboldt-Toiyabe National Forest, 4701 N. Torrey Pines Dr., Las Vegas 89130-2301; (702) 872-5486; https://www.fs.usda.gov/htnf

Finding the trailhead: From the intersection of US 95 and I-15 in downtown Las Vegas, drive 16.7 miles northwest on US 95. Turn left on NV 157, Kyle Canyon Road, and drive 17.5 miles. Turn right on NV 158 and drive 4.9 miles to the North Loop Trailhead, on the left. GPS: N36 18.528'/W115 36.691'

The Hike

The North Loop Trail first skirts the edge of the road cut above the highway, then turns south and climbs steadily through stands of mountain mahogany, ponderosa pine, piñon pine, and juniper. As the slope steepens, the trail begins to switchback, and soon the first limber pine, white fir, and bristlecone pines appear. As the North Loop Trail comes out onto a windswept point, bristlecone pines begin to dominate the forest. A switchback on the end of the ridge offers a sweeping view of the Las Vegas Valley. After leaving this open area behind, the trail climbs through denser forest, and finally tops out on the end of another ridge. Now the trail descends gradually, passing through two saddles. At the second saddle, watch for a faint, unmarked hiker trail going left, just before the low point of the saddle.

Fletcher Peak is visible to the left as you arrive at this saddle. Follow the informal trail across the hillside toward Fletcher Peak and down into a saddle. The trail, marked by cairns, works its way around several minor rocky knobs and up to the summit. A second summit of Fletcher Peak is visible just to the east. The view is expansive in all directions, including the imposing cliffs of Mummy Mountain near at hand to the

Bristlecone pine has purplish cones covered with bristles and short, stiff needles that grow in tight bunches of five.

north, the Sheep Range to the north, Kyle Canyon to the west, and the long ridge running south from Charleston Peak.

Every outdoor guidebook, including this one, warns you to get off ridges and high points during thunderstorms. The number of lightning-struck trees you see on a ridge such as the one leading to Fletcher Peak make the danger obvious. Such exposed areas are dangerous, but open areas where you are the primary target are much more hazardous. This is borne out by the fact that many more golfers than hikers get struck by lightning. Golf courses are open, with at most isolated clumps of trees, and there's no safe place to go. Isolated trees are very dangerous places to wait out a storm because they tend to attract lightning strikes.

The only truly safe place to go during lightning is an enclosed, protected space, such as a car or a building with lightning rods, but such shelter is not available in the backcountry. The best tactic when caught out on a hike by lightning is to make yourself as small of a target as possible. To do this, it helps to understand how lightning strikes.

Lightning is a huge spark of static electricity that jumps between two charged clouds, or a charged cloud and the ground. As a thunderstorm builds up overhead, vertical wind currents act like a giant electrical generator, building up an electric charge in the cloud. As this happens an opposite charge builds up in the ground below the cloud. When the voltage builds up high enough to overcome the insulating effect of the air, a lightning bolt leaps between the cloud and the ground, discharging the built-up charge.

> Evergreen trees growing high in the mountains have adapted to the harsh winters and heavy snows in several ways. Most alpine trees have densely bunched needles to conserve warmth. This is especially evident in the "bottle-brush" appearance of bristlecone pine branches. Another adaptation becomes obvious when you push your way past a limber pine. This well-named tree has extremely flexible branches, which help it withstand and shed heavy snow loads without breaking.

Studies have shown that as the charge builds to the critical point, invisible leaders descend from the cloud base. Similar leaders rise from points on the ground toward the cloud. The leaders are essentially areas of the highest voltage where the air is starting to break down and lose its insulating ability. Ben Franklin, the inventor of the lightning rod, discovered that voltages are highest at the tips of sharp objects, such as treetops, flagpoles, and radio towers. So ground leaders tend to develop from the highest, most exposed points in the landscape. For hikers, that means sharp summits and, even more importantly, treetops.

Many hundreds of leaders develop from cloud and ground, but the first two to meet instantly create a path for the charge to travel, and a lightning strike occurs. A strike is actually many separate discharges all happening in a fraction of a second, which is why lightning flickers. The strikes may travel from cloud to ground or the reverse, but the effect is the same. Hundreds of thousands of volts cause hundreds of thousands of amps of current to flow through the object on the ground. This is more than enough to electrocute a hiker, flash tree sap into steam, and set fires. Yet most lightning-strike victims are not actually struck directly by the lightning bolt. Instead they are injured by ground currents. Understanding ground currents greatly increases your safety during lightning storms.

The voltage and current from a lightning strike dissipates over the area around the object that was struck, creating a voltage gradient that extends a few dozen feet from the center of the strike. Over this distance the voltage decreases from hundreds of thousands of volts to zero. Voltage is what drives electrical current through an object, and current is what causes damage and injury. An ordinary flashlight battery

ROUTE-FINDING SKILLS

The trick to following a cairned (piles of rocks) or blazed (a mark cut into a tree at chest height) route is to always keep the last cairn or blaze in sight while you look for the next one. This is especially important in places where the route might suddenly veer off in an unexpected direction. Such places as saddles, forks on ridges, and heads of drainages are common places where a route will abruptly change direction. If you can't find the next cairn or blaze, backtrack to the last marker and search around it in the most likely directions while always keeping the last marker in sight.

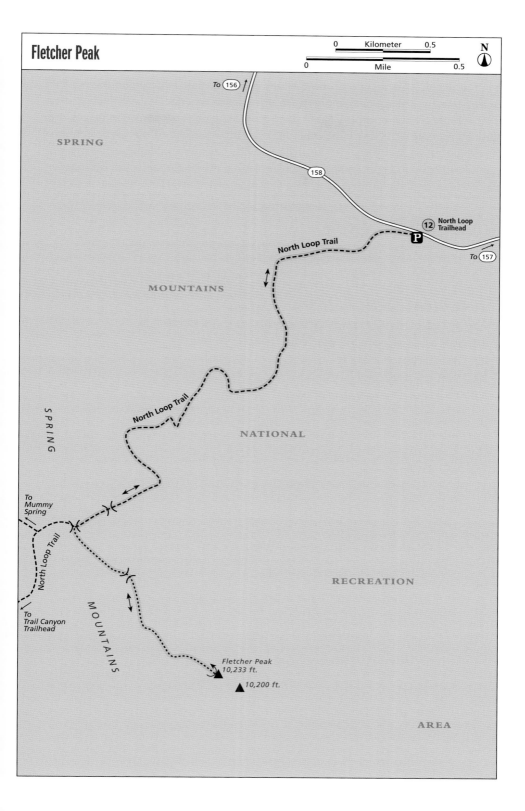

Fletcher Peak

0   Kilometer   0.5

0   Mile   0.5

N

SPRING

To 156

158

MOUNTAINS

North Loop Trail

12 North Loop Trailhead

P

To 157

North Loop Trail

SPRING

NATIONAL

To Mummy Spring

North Loop Trail

RECREATION

To Trail Canyon Trailhead

MOUNTAINS

Fletcher Peak 10,233 ft.

▲ 10,200 ft.

AREA

has more than enough current to kill a person, but lacks the voltage to overcome skin resistance.

If a person is standing with his feet about a foot apart when lightning strikes a nearby tree, the voltage gradient between the feet can easily be 10,000 volts or more. This is more than enough voltage to drive a damaging electrical current up one leg, through the torso, and down the other leg. To reduce the hazard, stay away from isolated high points and trees, and squat down with your feet as close together as you can. If you have a sleeping pad or other insulation, put that under your feet. Stay in this position until the thunderstorm and lightning have moved away. People in groups should spread out to minimize the chances of more than one person being struck.

Miles and Directions

0.0 Leave the North Loop Trailhead and start on the North Loop Trail.

1.2 The North Loop Trail reaches a ridge with windblown bristlecone pines and a view to the northeast.

2.0 At the first saddle, continue on the North Loop Trail.

2.1 At the second saddle, turn left on a faint hiker trail toward Fletcher Peak.

2.3 Pass through a saddle and start the final ascent of the peak.

2.8 Fletcher Peak; return the way you came.

3.5 Meet up with the North Loop Trail and turn right, retracing your steps.

5.6 Arrive back at the North Loop Trailhead.

14 Bristlecone Loop

This trail circles an unnamed hill at the head of Lee Canyon and passes through an extensive stand of ancient bristlecone pines. This is one of the few trails in the Spring Mountains that is open to mountain bikers, and it makes a fine ride.

Start: 47.9 miles northwest of Las Vegas
Distance: 5.6-mile loop
Approximate hiking time: 4 hours
Difficulty: Moderate due to 1,100-foot elevation gain
Trail surface: Dirt and rocks, old roads, 0.4-mile section of paved highway to close the loop
Best seasons: Spring through fall
Water: None
Other trail users: Horses and mountain bikes

Canine compatibility: Leashed dogs permitted
Fees and permits: None
Schedule: All year
Maps: CalTopo.com MapBuilder Topo layer; USGS Charleston Peak
Trail contacts: Spring Mountains National Recreation Area, Humboldt-Toiyabe National Forest, 4701 N. Torrey Pines Dr., Las Vegas 89130-2301; (702) 872-5486; https://www.fs.usda.gov/htnf

Finding the trailhead: From the intersection of US 95 and I-15 in downtown Las Vegas, drive 30.2 miles northwest on US 95. Turn left on NV 156, Lee Canyon Road. Continue 17.7 miles to the Upper Bristlecone Trailhead at the end of the highway, across from the Las Vegas Ski and Snowboard Resort. GPS: N36 18.407'/W115 40.687'

The Hike

At first the trail heads southwest along a ridge above the ski area. A fence on both sides of the trail was erected to protect some of the fragile, endemic plants that grow here. Soon the trail drops into a canyon bottom filled with an alpine forest of white fir, Douglas fir, bristlecone pines, and aspen. After the Bristlecone Trail makes a sharp right turn and climbs out of the canyon to the north, it crosses a more exposed slope where living conditions are much tougher than the canyon bottom you just left. These are exactly the conditions that bristlecone pines favor. In fact the Spring Mountains have extensive stands of bristlecones—at some 18,000 acres, the largest stand of bristlecones anywhere. Bristlecone pines are easy to identify by their needles, which grow in tight groups of five, giving the branches a "bottlebrush" appearance.

Bristlecone pines actually do grow well below timberline, where they are taller and more slender than their gnarled timberline counterparts. But the

▶ Plants that reproduce by cloning, such as the quaking aspen and creosote bush, have been dated at more than 10,000 years old. The distinction is that all the succeeding generations are genetically identical, but unlike bristlecone pines, they are not the same individual plant.

Bristlecone pines live longest on exposed ridges where the growing conditions are the harshest.

easy living exacts a price: "Low elevation" bristlecone pines rarely live 1,000 years before succumbing to disease, rot, or insects.

Descending slightly to a saddle, the trail reaches the end of a now-abandoned road built by the Works Project Administration during the 1930s. The WPA and its sister "alphabet agencies" provided employment for thousands of people during the Great Depression and constructed roads, trails, bridges, and campgrounds throughout the national forests. At a saddle the Bristlecone Trail meets the Bonanza Trail; stay right on the Bristlecone Trail. The trail continues to descend, and the broad roadbed allows for some fine views.

Continue on the Bristlecone Trail as it heads east along the south slopes of a ridge. The trail swings around the east end of this ridge and descends into Scout Canyon in one long switchback to the west. The trail then turns east, and then south to end at the Lower Bristlecone Trailhead. Walk a short distance down the dirt road to NV 156, then follow the highway south to the Upper Bristlecone Trailhead.

Bristlecone pines are the patriarchs of the Southwestern forests, and their gnarled appearance reinforces that impression. Bristlecone pines are the oldest living trees anywhere and among the oldest living things on earth. Currently, the oldest known bristlecone pine is the Methuselah Tree in the White Mountains on the Nevada–California border, dated at 4,851 years old. An older tree was found in the Snake

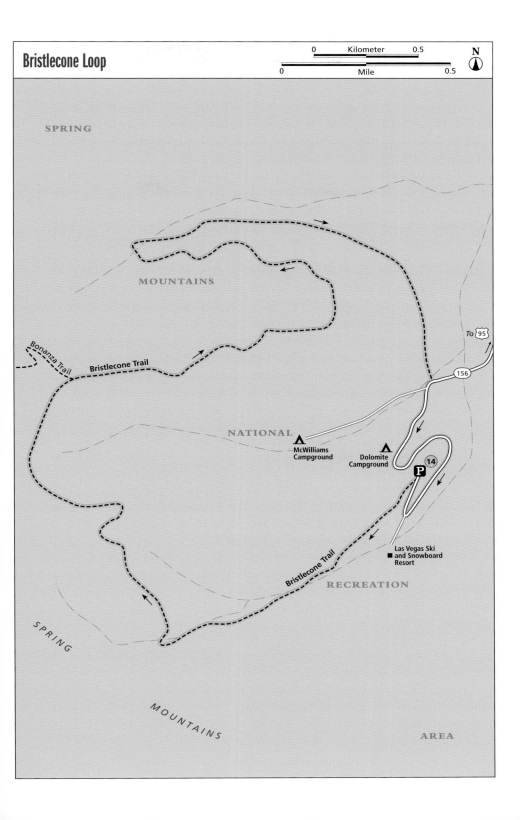

Bristlecone Loop

SPRING

MOUNTAINS

Bonanza Trail

Bristlecone Trail

NATIONAL

McWilliams
Campground

Dolomite
Campground

To 95

156

14

P

Las Vegas Ski
and Snowboard
Resort

Bristlecone Trail

RECREATION

SPRING

MOUNTAINS

AREA

0   Kilometer   0.5

0   Mile   0.5

N

Range in east-central Nevada, but its age—over 4,900 years old—was only discovered after it had been cut down for research purposes. Normally, trees are dated by taking core samples with a special coring tool that leaves the tree undamaged, but in this case the researcher's tree-coring tool broke before he could finish his summer research project. Not suspecting that the tree he was about to study was so old, he asked permission from the managing agency to cut down just this one tree with a chainsaw.

The age of such a tree boggles the imagination. The oldest bristlecone pines started their lives at the dawn of recorded human history, thousands of miles away in the Middle East, and have lived through all the events since then. Wars have raged and civilizations have fallen while the trees clung to life in some of the most inhospitable places on earth—timberline on isolated mountain ranges in the middle of a desert.

Young bristlecone pines, those that have only reached 1,500 years or so in age, grow in the same fashion as other conifers, with a single, roundish central trunk covered with bark and living cambium. Bristlecone pines growing in sheltered forests below timberline grow straight and tall but rarely live more than 1,000 years before succumbing to heart rot. Timberline trees are short and gnarled, and older trees may be 5 feet thick and only 10 or 15 feet tall. As the tree ages, the roots become exposed by erosion and dry out, leaving the tree with less ability to support a full crown of branches. The tree's tactic is strip growth, where much of the cambium dies and the bark falls away, leaving most of the circumference of the trunk bare wood. Only a strip of bark may run up the trunk, providing nutrients to a few living branches. Under that living strip, new wood is added very slowly, and the new wood is exceptionally dense and resinous. The bristlecone not only needs very little water and soil to survive, but also creates wood that is very resistant to decay and attack by insects.

The type of soil makes a difference also. Bristlecone pines grow well on granite and quartzite-derived soils, but the oldest trees grow on dolomite, as found in the White Mountains of California and Nevada. The limestone and dolomite found on the high ridges of the Spring Mountains are a favorable environment, which is one reason the bristlecone stands are so extensive here.

There appear to be several reasons that dolomite and limestone are such advantageous environments for bristlecone pines. These calcite rocks form poor soil, and plants are widely spaced. Young bristlecone pines need a lot of light to support their early fast growth, so they may favor dolomite and limestone because of the lack of competition. Also, light-colored dolomite and limestone reflect more light than darker rocks, which provides more light for the tree's photosynthesis, as well as keeping soil moisture and temperatures up. Slight increases in soil moisture make a large difference in the young bristlecone's rate of growth.

Because it is so resistant to decay, dead bristlecone wood lasts a long time—one piece more than 9,000 years old has been found (one good reason why you should never build campfires at timberline). By correlating tree rings between living and dead bristlecone wood, the tree ring record can be extended thousands of years into the past, giving researchers a window into past environments and climate.

Miles and Directions

0.0 Leave the Upper Bristlecone Trailhead on the Bristlecone Trail.

1.0 The Bristlecone Trail turns abruptly right (north) and leaves the canyon.

1.8 Cross the high point of the loop.

2.0 The singletrack trail becomes an old, closed road.

2.3 You'll reach the junction with the Bonanza Trail in a saddle; stay right to remain on the Bristlecone Trail.

3.2 The Bristlecone Trail crosses a ridge and starts to descend into Scout Canyon.

4.0 The trail arrives in the bottom of Scout Canyon and turns sharply right.

5.2 Arrive at Lower Bristlecone Trailhead. Follow the dirt road a few yards to NV 156, then follow the highway south to the Upper Bristlecone Trailhead.

5.6 Arrive back at the Upper Bristlecone Trailhead.

15 Sawmill Loop

On the approach road to Lee Canyon, this easy trail loops through piñon–juniper woodland and through open meadows that offer views of the high peaks above Lee Canyon.

Start: 43.3 miles northwest of Las Vegas
Distance: 1.3-mile loop
Approximate hiking time: 1 hour
Difficulty: Easy due to no elevation change
Trail surface: Dirt and rocks
Best season: All year
Water: None
Other trail users: Horses and mountain bikes
Canine compatibility: Leashed dogs permitted

Fees and permits: None
Schedule: All year
Maps: CalTopo.com MapBuilder Topo layer; USGS Charleston Peak
Trail contacts: Spring Mountains National Recreation Area, Humboldt-Toiyabe National Forest, 4701 N. Torrey Pines Dr., Las Vegas 89130-2301; (702) 872-5486; https://www.fs.usda.gov/htnf

Finding the trailhead: From the intersection of US 95 and I-15 in downtown Las Vegas, drive 30.2 miles northwest on US 95. Turn left on NV 156, Lee Canyon Road. Continue 13.1 miles to the Sawmill Trailhead, on the right. Park at the left end of the parking area, at the hiker trailhead. GPS: N36 21.296' / W115 38.475'

The Hike

As you leave the parking area on the Sawmill Trail, you immediately come to a junction. Turn right to start the loop hike. The trail wanders through dense stands of piñon pine and juniper, with scraggly cliffrose scattered throughout. As the trail twists and turns and passes through openings in the woodland, you'll get views of the peaks at the head of Lee Canyon. As you continue around the loop, the trail climbs gradually, and then descends gently to return to the trailhead.

Piñon–juniper woodland, as found along the Sawmill Trail, covers vast areas of the Intermountain West at intermediate elevations. Strangely enough, piñon and juniper become less common as you cross Nevada to the northwest, and disappear entirely just northwest of Winnemucca, even though the habitat on the mountainsides seems favorable. One theory is that piñon–juniper disappeared from all of Nevada during the cooler climate of the last glacial period, and returned from the east when the climate turned warmer. According to this theory, piñon–juniper is still spreading to the northwest.

Another theory is that the lack of summer moisture limits the range of the piñon–juniper woodland. In Nevada, summer rain comes mainly in the form of afternoon thunderstorms triggered by the late summer flow of monsoon moisture from the Gulf of Mexico. The monsoon rarely reaches northwestern Nevada, and summers are hot and dry. In contrast, in southeastern Nevada where the monsoon is moderate in intensity, piñon-juniper woodland is common. Further south and east, in northern Arizona and in New Mexico where the monsoon is stronger, piñon-juniper woodland covers vast areas of the plateaus and valleys as well as lower mountain slopes.

In the Spring Mountains, piñon-juniper covers the lower slopes of the range. The two main trees that make up this woodland are singleleaf piñon pine and Utah juniper. Other plants that grow in association are cliffrose, unmistakable in late spring when it is covered with hundreds of small, white, fragrant flowers, and flowers such as Indian paintbrush, also unmistakable with its bright red brushlike flowers.

Utah juniper grows only 10 to 15 feet high, and singleleaf piñon pine reaches a maximum height of about 50 feet in favored locations, though it is usually 15 to 20 feet high. Piñon pines need slightly more moisture than junipers, so they favor the upper portion of the piñon-juniper belt, and junipers are more numerous at the lower limits. The woodland varies from fairly dense where the conditions are favorable, as along the Sawmill Trail, to open stands at the lower limit.

Many animals, such as mule deer, coyotes, and bobcats, make the piñon-juniper woodland their home. One particular bird stands out in this pygmy forest: the piñon jay. When no other birds are present, you'll see the pale blue jays flitting from tree to tree, and their soft *eeee* calls are even more obvious. Piñon jays are entirely dependent on the pine nuts of the piñon pine for their survival. Since a given grove of piñons only bears cones every few years, piñon jays collect the nuts during good years and stash them in hidden caches for use during the winter and lean summers. Typically, the birds bury their caches a few inches deep. One bird makes hundreds of such caches,

Flowers grow among the sage and piñon-juniper woodland along the Sawmill Trail.

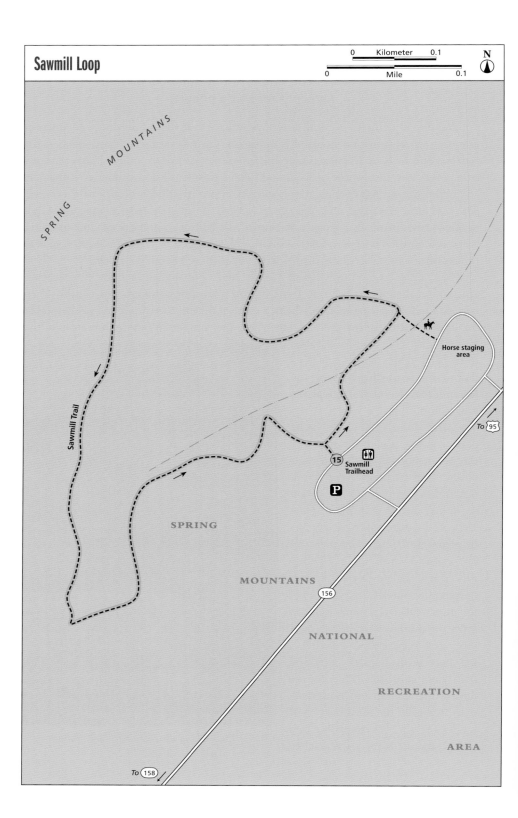

and then finds most of them with uncanny precision, even when the ground is covered with a few inches of snow.

Researchers have had a hard time understanding how a creature with such a tiny brain can store all the information required to locate hundreds of caches with an accuracy of better than 90 percent. One theory is that the birds store mental maps of the caches with ever-increasing detail as they get closer to the cache, much as a computer user zooms in on a map on the screen.

The few caches that are not found are vital for the piñon pine, as missed caches are the primary method by which the piñon pine is propagated over long distances. The piñon jay literally gives the piñon pine wings.

Early human inhabitants were also major users of the piñon pine nut. Nomadic groups such as the Paiute would wander in clan-size groups in search of game and plants most of the year, but during the pine nut harvest, they would gather in sizable villages along mountain slopes where there was a good crop. After the harvest was over, the clans would split up and go their separate ways. Modern people also love pine nuts, and those from the American Southwest's singleleaf piñon are especially prized.

Miles and Directions

0.0 From the west end of the parking area, start the hike on the Sawmill Trail. After just a few yards, turn right at a signed junction to start the loop.

0.2 The trail from the horse-staging area joins from the right; stay left on the main Sawmill loop.

0.5 Pass the high point of the loop on a slightly steeper hillside.

0.9 The trail turns east and northeast back toward the trailhead.

1.3 Arrive at a signed trail junction; turn right, and walk a few yards to the Sawmill Trailhead.

16 Bonanza Peak

This hike ascends 10,380-foot Bonanza Peak using the Bonanza Trail and a short, easy cross-country hike. Bonanza Peak is the northernmost 10,000-foot peak in the Spring Mountains and has a commanding view of the Spring Mountains from an unusual perspective. Though not much farther from the city than the popular Lee and Kyle Canyon areas, you'll see far fewer people in this remote portion of the national recreation area.

Start: 52.0 miles northwest of Las Vegas
Distance: 7.8 miles out and back
Approximate hiking time: 6 hours
Difficulty: Strenuous due to 2,900-foot elevation change and high elevations
Trail surface: Dirt and rocks, cross-country
Best seasons: Spring through fall
Water: None
Other trail users: Horses
Canine compatibility: Leashed dogs permitted

Fees and permits: None
Schedule: Open all hours
Maps: CalTopo.com MapBuilder Topo layer; USGS Cold Creek, Willow Peak, Wheeler Well, Charleston Peak
Trail contacts: Spring Mountains National Recreation Area, Humboldt-Toiyabe National Forest, 4701 N. Torrey Pines Dr., Las Vegas 89130-2301; (702) 872-5486; https://www .fs.usda.gov/htnf

Finding the trailhead: From the intersection of US 95 and I-15 in downtown Las Vegas, drive 35.9 miles on US 95. Turn right on Cold Creek Road and continue 16.1 miles to the end of the road at the Bonanza Trailhead. Toward the end you'll pass through a subdivision; stay on Cold Creek Road. After passing the subdivision the road becomes gravel for the last 2.0 miles and is passable by ordinary cars with care. GPS: N36 22.947'/W115 44.439'

The Hike

The Bonanza Trail climbs away from the trailhead to the southwest, passing through stands of mountain mahogany and ponderosa pine. It soon begins to switchback up a broad ridge at an easy but relentless grade. As the trail continues to climb, the magnificent old-growth ponderosa pines are joined by white and Douglas firs. About halfway up the ascent, the north end of a switchback comes to the edge of the old fire that burned over the top of Willow Peak, giving views of the limestone cliffs of Willow Peak itself and the desert far beyond to the north.

As you climb, watch for the first appearance of bristlecone pines. This five-needled pine is joined by another, limber pine, which has longer needles in more open bunches. As the name implies, limber pine has flexible branches that allow it to shed heavy snow loads. More switchbacks finally lead to a saddle on the edge of the burn, on the ridge between Willow and Bonanza Peaks.

Continue on the Bonanza Trail to the south as it climbs the ridge above the saddle, soon entering an unburned forest of bristlecone pines. Switchbacks lead up the west side of the ridge, and when the trail levels out and starts to descend along the slopes of Bonanza Peak, leave the trail and walk directly up to the peak. The summit itself is a small rocky knob with views to the north, east, and south. Charleston Peak is visible to the southeast at the head of Kyle Canyon, as are the summits at the head of Lee Canyon.

The burn on the northeast slopes of Willow Peak is in the early stages of forest succession. When a forest is destroyed by a natural or man-made disaster such as a snow avalanche, landslide, windstorm, flood, or wild fire, the forest immediately begins to restore itself.

Forest succession varies with the forest type and the climate, but the same general process is always followed. The first step is soil recovery, in the case of a flood or forest fire where the soil may be covered or destroyed. A lot of changes take place that are hidden within the soil, caused by beneficial microbes, fungi, and burrowing creatures such as earthworms. That sets the stage for the first visible plants to take hold. Grass and brush are usually the first plants to grow on the diminished soil left in the wake of the event. As more plants grow, they enrich the soil, and eventually the soil is capable of supporting the first trees.

From the summit of Bonanza Peak, the northernmost 10,000-foot peak in the Spring Mountains, you can get a different perspective of Charleston Peak and the central part of the range.

CROWN FIRES

The fire on the east side of Willow Peak is an example of a crown fire. These fires occur in dry, windy conditions and are aggravated by unnatural forest conditions such as heavy accumulations of dead plant material on the forest floor. If enough heat is generated, the fire may change from a low-intensity ground fire, which is generally beneficial to the forest, to a high-intensity crown fire where the fire moves rapidly through the treetops, killing the trees and almost every living thing in its path. Such fires in heavy timber can release the same energy as a nuclear explosion every few minutes.

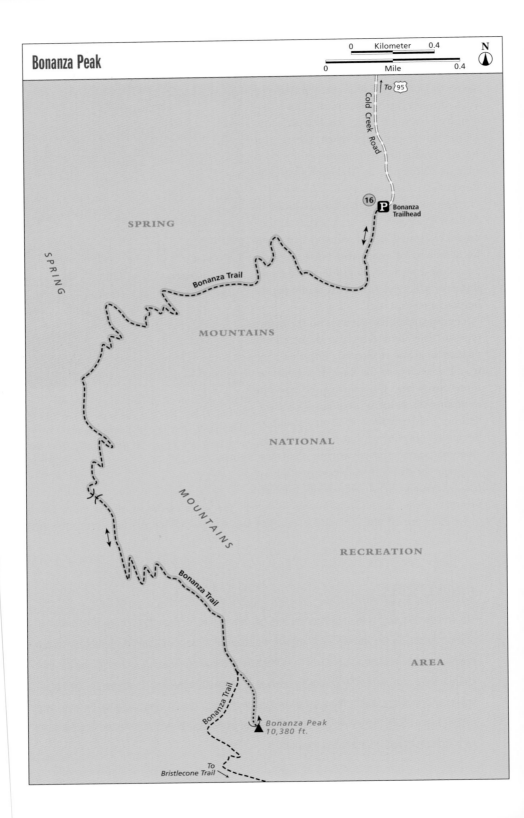

Bonanza Peak

0   Kilometer   0.4

0   Mile   0.4

N

To 95

Cold Creek Road

16 P Bonanza Trailhead

SPRING

SPRING

Bonanza Trail

MOUNTAINS

NATIONAL

MOUNTAINS

RECREATION

Bonanza Trail

AREA

Bonanza Trail

▲ Bonanza Peak
10,380 ft.

To
Bristlecone Trail

On higher slopes quaking aspen is usually the first tree to become established. Aspen requires a lot of sunlight, and open burned slopes are ideal sites once the soil is thick enough and rich enough to support tree roots. Aspen grows quickly, and old burns are often covered with 10-foot-tall young aspen trees within a few years.

As the aspens mature, they provide shade for evergreens such as Douglas and white fir, whose seedlings can't withstand intense sunlight. It may take a hundred years or more, but eventually the evergreens grow taller than the aspens and begin to deprive them of the sunlight they need. At the same time, the aspens are dying of old age—aspens don't live much longer than one hundred years. The end result is a new evergreen mountain forest.

Such a forest was once referred to as a "climax forest," meaning the final and stable forest type. Today it's recognized that forests are always in flux, and there isn't necessarily a final stage.

Miles and Directions

0.0 Leave the Bonanza Trailhead on the Bonanza Trail.

1.7 View the burn on Willow Peak; continue on the Bonanza Trail.

2.7 Reach a saddle on the ridge between Willow and Bonanza Peaks; continue south on the Bonanza Trail.

3.7 Leave the trail and follow a faint hiker trail up the south ridge of Bonanza Peak, keeping just to the right of the rocky ridge crest until just below the summit.

3.9 Bonanza Peak; return the way you came.

7.8 Arrive back at the Bonanza Trailhead.

17 Bonanza Trail

Linking the Bonanza Trailhead to the Upper Bristlecone Trailhead, this hike follows the crest of the northwestern Spring Mountains and offers rare glimpses of one of the most remote portions of the Spring Mountains.

Start: 52.0 miles northwest of Las Vegas
Distance: 15.9 miles one-way with a car shuttle
Approximate hiking time: 9–10 hours or overnight backpack trip
Difficulty: Strenuous due to 2,900-foot elevation change and high elevations
Trail surface: Dirt and rocks, a short section of old road on the Bristlecone Trail
Best seasons: Spring through fall
Water: Seasonal at Wood Spring
Other trail users: Horses; mountain bikes on the Bristlecone Trail
Canine compatibility: Leashed dogs permitted

Fees and permits: None
Schedule: Open all hours
Maps: CalTopo.com MapBuilder Topo layer; USGS Cold Creek, Willow Peak, Wheeler Well, Charleston Peak
Trail contacts: Spring Mountains National Recreation Area, Humboldt-Toiyabe National Forest, 4701 N. Torrey Pines Dr., Las Vegas 89130-2301; (702) 872-5486; https://www.fs.usda.gov/htnf
Special considerations: For backpackers the best time to do this hike is during late spring or early summer right after snowmelt, when you'll have the best chance of finding water.

Finding the trailhead: *Ending point at Upper Bristlecone Trailhead:* From the intersection of US 95 and I-15 in downtown Las Vegas, drive 30.2 miles northwest on US 95. Turn left on NV 156, Lee Canyon Road. Continue 17.7 miles to the Upper Bristlecone Trailhead at the end of the highway, across from the Las Vegas Ski and Snowboard Resort. GPS: N36 18.407'/W115 40.687'

Starting point at the Bonanza Trailhead: From the Upper Bristlecone Trailhead, drive 17.1 miles on NV 156. Turn left on US 95 and drive 5.7 miles northwest. Turn right on Cold Creek Road and continue 16.1 miles to the end of the road at the Bonanza Trailhead. Toward the end, you'll pass through a subdivision; stay on Cold Creek Road. After passing the subdivision the road becomes gravel for the last 2.0 miles and is passable by ordinary cars with care. GPS: N36 22.947'/W115 44.439'

The Hike

The Bonanza Trail climbs away from the trailhead to the southwest, passing through stands of mountain mahogany and ponderosa pine. It soon begins to switchback up a broad ridge at an easy but relentless grade. As the trail continues to climb, the

GREEN TIP:
When backpacking, use a camp stove instead of building a fire. In these mountains the wood you're burning may have started life before the dawn of human civilization.

The Bonanza Trail winds along the crest of the northern Spring Mountains, more than 7,000 feet above the deserts below.

magnificent old-growth ponderosa pines are joined by white and Douglas firs. About halfway up the ascent, the north end of a switchback comes to the edge of the old fire that burned over the top of Willow Peak, giving views of the limestone cliffs of Willow Peak itself and the desert far beyond to the north.

As you climb, watch for the first appearance of bristlecone pines. This five-needle pine is joined by another, limber pine, which has longer needles in more open bunches. As the name implies, limber pine has flexible branches that allow it to shed heavy snow loads. More switchbacks finally lead to a saddle on the edge of the burn, on the ridge between Willow and Bonanza Peaks.

Continue on the Bonanza Trail to the south as it climbs the ridge above the saddle, soon entering an unburned forest of bristlecone pines. Switchbacks lead up the west side of the ridge, and then the trail levels out and starts to descend along the slopes of Bonanza Peak. A series of switchbacks descend to Wood Spring, and then the Bonanza Trail descends more gently.

The trail more or less contours around the west and south sides of rugged McFarland Peak, and then more switchbacks lead up the ridge southeast of the peak. After regaining the ridge crest, the Bonanza Trail follows the crest southeast and south, bypassing a

▶ **When backpacking in these desert mountains, where water sources are few and far between, consider using collapsible plastic water containers. The current generation of bottles is reliable and extremely lightweight. Plus, you have the capacity to carry a lot of water when you need to, and the empties take up little room in your pack.**

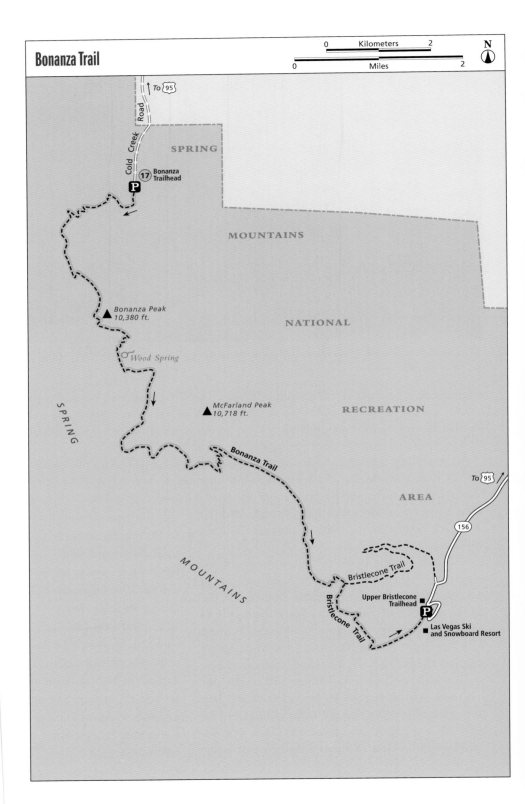

Bonanza Trail

To 95

Cold Creek Road

SPRING

17 Bonanza Trailhead

P

MOUNTAINS

▲ Bonanza Peak
10,380 ft.

SPRING

Wood Spring

McFarland Peak
10,718 ft.

NATIONAL

RECREATION

Bonanza Trail

To 95

156

AREA

MOUNTAINS

Bristlecone Trail

Bristlecone Trail

Upper Bristlecone
Trailhead

P

Las Vegas Ski
and Snowboard Resort

continues, the sandstone dom become isolated, with expanses of flat rock or sand in between.

Slickrock country can seem chaotic because of the joint canyons that seem to run every which way, but the fact that running water is the main agent of erosion imposes order on the landscape. Every tiny drainage leads to a larger one, which in turn leads to a larger one, and so on until (in this case) the runoff reaches the Overton Arm of Lake Mead, the former course of the Virgin River, which in turn flows into the Colorado River and to the sea.

Sometimes the effect of joints can be seen when they are still buried. Flat expanses of sandstone often have a thin layer of soil or sand. In such areas plants can be seen growing in straight lines as if manually planted there. What's happening is that the plants tend to grow along the slightly buried joints because moisture tends to collect along the hidden cracks.

▶ While most of the sandstone formations in the Valley of Fire are red, white sandstone is predominant in the White Domes area. Color variations in the sandstone are caused by slight mineral impurities that stain the fine grains of quartz. Red rocks are generally the result of trace amounts of iron oxide (rust), and white rocks lack coloration, letting the natural white color of the quartz grains show.

Joint canyons can be truly impressive—straight as an arrow and sometimes hundreds of feet deep. Often the floor of the joint canyon is covered with loose sand, so the fact that water widened the joint is not obvious. Many years may pass between

Red rock sandstone formations rise like stone ships out of the desert flats.

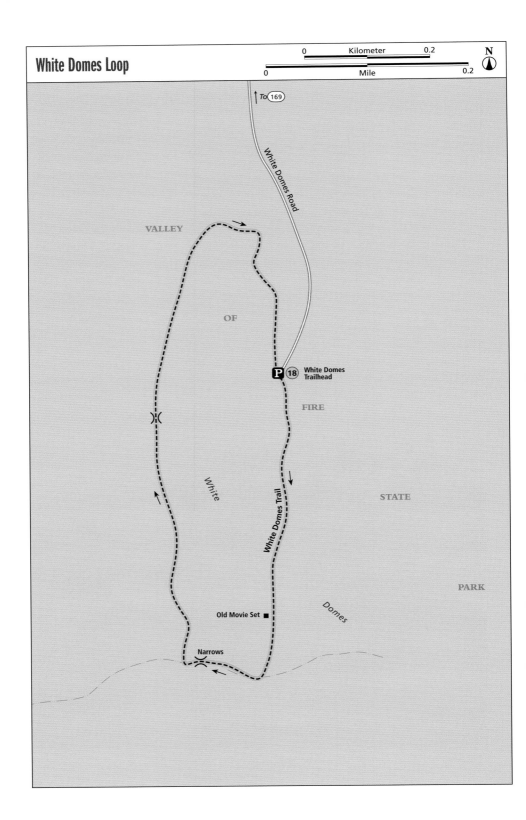

White Domes Loop

0 Kilometer 0.2
0 Mile 0.2

N

To 169

White Domes Road

VALLEY

OF

P 18 White Domes Trailhead

FIRE

White

White Domes Trail

STATE

PARK

Domes

Old Movie Set ■

Narrows

major rainstorms in any given desert area so that erosion proceeds at a very slow pace and drifting sand tends to obscure the fact that the joint is a watercourse. Also remember that the landscape evolves over geologic time, where a human lifetime is but an instant.

Miles and Directions

0.0 Start the loop clockwise by hiking south on the White Domes Trail from the trail sign at the south end of the parking lot.

0.4 Pass the old movie set, turn right, and follow the trail west down the wash.

0.7 At the end of the narrows, follow the trail north over a low pass.

1.0 The White Domes Trail turns right and heads east.

1.1 Follow the trail south.

1.2 Arrive back at the White Domes Trailhead.

19 Rainbow Vista Trail

This trail leads across sand dunes and through red rock canyons to an overlook above the rugged depths of Fire Canyon.

Start: 53.1 miles northeast of Las Vegas
Distance: 1.1 miles out and back
Approximate hiking time: 1 hour
Difficulty: Easy due to no elevation change
Trail surface: Sand
Best seasons: Fall through spring
Water: None
Other trail users: None
Canine compatibility: Leashed dogs permitted, maximum 6-foot leash

Fees and permits: Entrance fee
Schedule: Open all hours
Maps: CalTopo.com MapBuilder Topo layer; USGS Valley of Fire West
Trail contacts: Valley of Fire State Park, 29450 Valley of Fire Rd., Overton 89040; (702) 397-2088; http://parks.nv.gov/parks/valley-of-fire
Special considerations: During the summer hike early in the day and carry plenty of water.

Finding the trailhead: From the intersection of US 95 and I-15 in downtown Las Vegas, drive 32.8 miles north on I-15. Turn right on NV 169, the Valley of Fire Highway, and drive 19.0 miles. Turn left on the road to the visitor center and Fire Canyon/White Domes. Continue past the visitor center 1.9 miles and park at the Rainbow Vista Trailhead, on the right. GPS: N36 27.058'/W114 30.922'

The Hike

From the Rainbow Vista Trailhead, the Rainbow Vista Trail heads southeast down a slope and then comes out into an open area of sand dunes. Turn left at a junction and follow a side trail that swings to the north across an open desert valley with a sweeping view to the north. This side trail soon rejoins the main trail; turn left and continue southeast. After walking through a passage between sandstone walls, you'll reach the end of the trail at a point overlooking the complex depths of Fire Canyon.

▶ **Many people think that slickrock formations such as the ones found in Valley of Fire are carved by wind. In reality nearly all of the erosion is done by water, strange as it may seem. Wind has only a minor effect, mainly that of moving loose sand around and forming dunes, and sandblasting exposed surfaces.**

To return, retrace your steps, except stay left at both junctions to return directly to the trailhead.

In slickrock country such as Valley of Fire, although water is the main agent of erosion, wind does move sand grains around, and if conditions are right, the loose sand collects into sand dunes. The right conditions include a steady supply of sand, reliable prevailing winds, and a collection area for the sand. Sand dunes move when the wind reaches about

12 to 15 miles per hour, the speed needed to pick up and transport the grains. Wind carries the sand up the windward face of the dune, and then drops its load abruptly on the lee side (the slip face). If you look at a dune from the side when the wind is just strong enough to transport sand, you can see a shallow layer, just an inch or two deep, flowing up the face of the dune. If the light is right, you can also see the sand being dropped on the slip face of the dune, and also see the tumbling, swirling air currents above the slip face.

The windward face slopes gently, while the lee face tends to be steeper, at the angle of repose for the sand (the steepest possible slope before the sand slides under its own weight). As sand is carried over the dune onto the slip face, the dune advances downwind. Because the sides of the dune have less sand to move, they tend to move faster than the main body,

Fire Canyon Overlook is the highlight of the Rainbow Vista Trail.

forming crescent-shaped dunes. Crescent dunes are the most common form of dune, forming in open country. White Sands National Monument in New Mexico is a classic area of crescent dunes.

While crescent dunes are the most common, constrictions in the topography such as along the Rainbow Vista Trail tend to form other types of dunes, or a mix of types. Linear dunes form downwind of a rim or other land feature that funnels the blowing sand into narrow streams, sometimes many miles long. Linear dunes can also form when the prevailing winds tend to reverse at certain times of the year.

When the wind blows from different directions, star dunes are common. These dunes tend to grow in height rather than moving. The Sahara Desert is the classic "sea of sand," which forms huge star dunes. Star dunes can reach more than 1,600 feet above their bases.

Dome dunes are small, rare dunes that sometimes appear at the ends of crescent-shaped dunes. They can also appear in constricted areas such as the first section of the Rainbow Vista Trail. Parabolic dunes are crescent-shaped in reverse, with arms

Rainbow Vista Trail

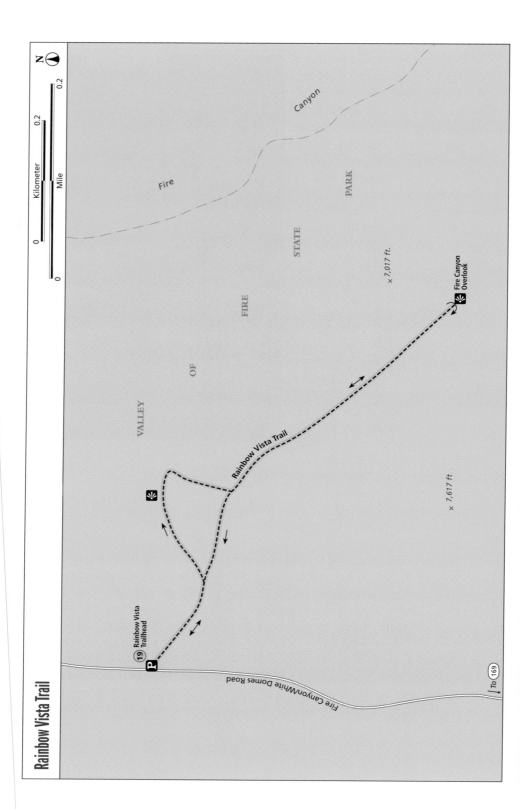

N

0   Kilometer   0.2

0   Mile   0.2

VALLEY OF FIRE STATE PARK

Fire Canyon

19 Rainbow Vista Trailhead

P

Rainbow Vista Trail

Fire Canyon/White Domes Road

To 169

x 7,017 ft.

x 7,617 ft

Fire Canyon Overlook

that point into the prevailing wind rather than away from it. The arms are usually anchored by vegetation.

Life being adaptable and tenacious, plants try to grow on sand dunes, but the shifting sand is a difficult environment. Fast-growing plants such as grasses have a better chance to become established than slower-growing plants such as brush. Once vegetation does get established, it anchors the dune and prevents further movement. In many areas dunes are partially anchored.

Miles and Directions

0.0 From the parking area, head southeast on the Rainbow Vista Trail.

0.1 Turn left on a side trail, which leads past a viewpoint facing north.

0.3 The side trail rejoins the main trail; turn left.

0.6 Reach Fire Canyon Overlook; return the way you came.

0.9 Stay left at the side trail junction.

1.0 Stay left at the second side trail junction.

1.1 Arrive back at the Rainbow Vista Trailhead.

20 Petroglyph Canyon

This hike takes you through a sandstone canyon featuring many panels of petro-glyphs. At the end you'll look out over a series of natural stone water tanks.

Start: 53.1 miles northeast of Las Vegas
Distance: 1.0 mile out and back
Approximate hiking time: 1 hour
Difficulty: Easy due to no elevation change
Trail surface: Sand
Best seasons: Fall through spring
Water: None
Other trail users: None
Canine compatibility: Leashed dogs permitted, maximum 6-foot leash

Fees and permits: Entrance fee
Schedule: Open all hours
Maps: CalTopo.com MapBuilder Topo layer; USGS Valley of Fire West
Trail contacts: Valley of Fire State Park, 29450 Valley of Fire Rd., Overton 89040; (702) 397-2088; http://parks.nv.gov/parks/valley-of-fire
Special considerations: During the summer hike early in the day and carry plenty of water.

Finding the trailhead: From the intersection of US 95 and I-15 in downtown Las Vegas, drive 32.8 miles north on I-15. Turn right on NV 169, the Valley of Fire Highway, and drive 19.0 miles. Turn left on the road to the visitor center and Fire Canyon/White Domes. Continue past the visitor center 1.3 miles and park at the Petroglyph Canyon / Mouse's Tank Trailhead, on the right. GPS: N36 26.463'/W114 30.974'

The Hike

From the trailhead the trail heads southeast into a small sandstone canyon. After you enter the canyon, watch for panels of rock art, or petroglyphs, mainly on the left side of the canyon. There are three main panels and several smaller ones. Just after the third panel, the trail turns sharply left and ends at Mouse's Tank, a series of stone basins that catch and hold runoff from the occasional rainstorms.

In the desert, where springs and streams are rare, water pockets and natural water tanks are vital water sources for wildlife and were also vital for the early human explorers and pioneers. Many travelers perished in the desert when they failed to find a water source in time. Though day hikers should carry all the water they need, this is not possible on an extended backpack trip. In some desert areas such as the Esplanade region of the Grand Canyon and the Canyonlands country of southeast Utah, multiday hiking trips are only possible and safe when recent rains have filled the water pockets and tanks.

A tank such as Mouse's Tank forms along a drainage when the action of flood-waters scours out the bed to form a depression, which usually happens at the base of pour-offs or dry waterfalls. Tanks can occur in sand and gravel, but they don't hold water for very long. The most enduring tanks are scoured out of bedrock at the bottom of narrow canyons. Less porous rocks such as granite retain water longer than

mature leaves and many of its twigs. The newest leaves are retained during dry periods and can survive a loss of 50 percent of their moisture. Photosynthesis continues during droughts so that the plant can immediately use any rain that arrives. Creosote's root system is shallow but extensive so that the plant can take advantage of fleeting soil moisture. The roots produce a germination inhibitor that prevents any creosote seedlings from growing within the root area. The inhibitor also prevents other plants from taking root and competing with the creosote for scarce water.

▶ Silica Dome is the location where the fight scene from the movie *Star Trek: Generations* was filmed, probably the most famous movie of the many that have been shot at Valley of Fire.

The creosote bush is also one of the longest-living plants. A single stem may live for a couple hundred years. The plant grows by producing new stems from the center of the root base, as older stems nearer the center die. The live stems form an expanding ring, and as hundreds of years pass, the ring breaks into separate plants, which are all clones of the original. It's estimated that the oldest creosotes are more than 11,000 years old, or as old as the Mohave Desert, which formed as the climate dried out and warmed after the last glacial period.

Barrel cactus looms above Fire Canyon, as seen from the short trail to Silica Dome.

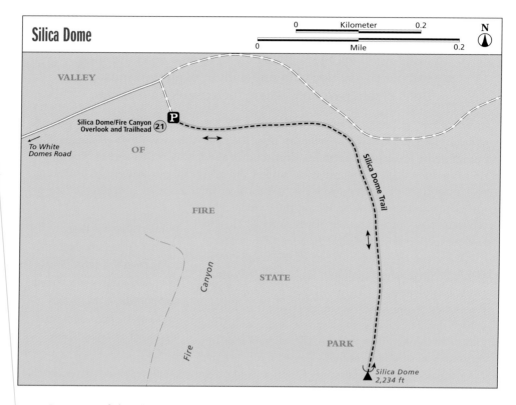

0   Kilometer   0.2

0   Mile   0.2

N

VALLEY

Silica Dome/Fire Canyon
Overlook and Trailhead (21) P

To White
Domes Road

OF

FIRE

Silica Dome Trail

Fire Canyon

STATE

PARK

Fire

Silica Dome
2,234 ft

In some of the driest areas, such as the Sonoran Desert around Yuma, Arizona, less than 3 inches of rain falls, and creosote is the only plant that survives in the most extreme areas. Creosote has been known to survive two years without rain.

Despite the barren appearance of the Mohave Desert, many other forms of life survive and even thrive here. Common plants include not only the creosote bush but also burro brush and brittle brush, typical Mohave Desert plants that cover large areas of the valleys and plains. Beavertail and cholla cactus are the most common cacti. Seasonal flowers that put on a show after wet winters include desert mallow, desert marigold, and indigo bush. Birds that live year-round in the park include roadrunners, house finches, ravens, and sage sparrow, in addition to migrating birds that travel through the park. There are many varieties of reptiles, including lizards and snakes, as well as the endangered desert tortoise. Mammals include coyotes, kit foxes, spotted skunks, black-tailed jackrabbits, ring-tailed cats, and antelope ground squirrels.

A lot of park visitors wonder why they don't see any wildlife, but then they are constantly on the move or talking to each other. Any noise or movement tends to

GREEN TIP:
Rechargeable (reusable) batteries reduce
one source of toxic garbage.

ORIGIN OF SILICA DOME

The name "Silica Dome" comes from the fact that sandstone is usually composed of tiny grains of quartz, a mineral primarily formed from silica. Quartz is a hard mineral and survives erosion that dissolves softer minerals. Sedimentary rocks such as those that make up Silica Dome are formed when silica sand grains are deposited in layers, usually underwater but occasionally in sand-dune fields. As more layers are deposited above and heat and pressure increases, the sand grains become cemented together with a mineral such as calcite and compressed into stone. Later, when the layers of sandstone are exposed by uplifting, water dissolves the calcite and carries away the sand grains, starting the process anew.

cause wildlife to move off. Using metal-tipped trekking poles virtually guarantees that you won't see any wildlife. Your best chance to see wildlife is to sit quietly in one place for a while, especially around sunset and sunrise.

Miles and Directions

0.0 Leave the Silica Dome Trailhead and hike east across a ravine.

0.2 When the trail meets an old road, turn right and head south, directly toward Silica Dome.

0.3 Start the climb by walking up easy sandstone slabs toward the summit.

0.4 Arrive at Silica Dome. Return the way you came.

0.8 Arrive back at the Silica Dome Trailhead.

22 Arrowhead Trail

A nice change from the sandy, slickrock trails in the Fire Canyon area, this trail follows a historic auto road through open desert.

Start: 47.8 miles northeast of Las Vegas
Distance: 12.0 miles out and back
Approximate hiking time: 6 hours
Difficulty: Moderate due to distance; little elevation change
Trail surface: Dirt and rocks
Best seasons: Fall through spring
Water: None
Other trail users: Horses
Canine compatibility: Leashed dogs permitted, maximum 6-foot leash

Fees and permits: Entrance fee
Schedule: Open all hours
Maps: CalTopo.com MapBuilder Topo layer; USGS Valley of Fire West, Valley of Fire East
Trail contacts: Valley of Fire State Park, 29450 Valley of Fire Rd., Overton 89040; (702) 397-2088; http://parks.nv.gov/parks/valley-of-fire
Special considerations: During the summer hike early in the day and carry plenty of water.

Finding the trailhead: From the intersection of US 95 and I-15 in downtown Las Vegas, drive 32.8 miles north on I-15. Turn right on the Valley of Fire Highway and drive 14.9 miles to the western Arrowhead Trailhead, a small pullout on the right. GPS: N36 24.485' / W114 33.430'

The Hike

From the pullout follow the Arrowhead Trail east. The old road is usually visible as two tracks, but occasionally disappears in sandy areas. It is well marked with stakes and easy to follow. The Arrowhead Trail passes south of Beehive Rock and then loosely follows a tributary of Valley of Fire Wash. After passing through a 0.25-mile-wide gap between rock formations, the valley opens out and the trail turns northeast along the dry wash. Just south of the visitor center, visible against the base of the cliffs to the left, the Arrowhead Trail turns eastward and follows Valley of Fire Wash. Finally, the trail turns to the northeast and meets the Valley of Fire Highway just east of Clark Memorial.

Valley of Fire State Park is in the Mohave Desert, the driest and hottest of the four North American deserts. A desert is defined as an area that receives less than 12 inches of annual precipitation on average. Parts of the Mohave Desert have gone years without any rainfall. Valley of Fire averages 4 inches of rain per year, mostly in the form of light winter rain and the occasional late-summer thunderstorm.

GREEN TIP:
Pack out what you pack in, even food scraps, because they can attract wild animals.

So why is this region a desert? In a word, mountains. Most storms come from the west (except for the summer monsoon), and to reach southern Nevada the storms must cross both the coast ranges and the lofty Sierra Nevada or the Cascade Mountains. As the moisture-laden air rises to cross the mountains, most of the moisture falls out of the clouds as snow or rain. The coast ranges are very wet on their upwind sides, as are the Sierra Nevada and Cascades. Downwind of these mountains, a "rain-shadow" desert forms, which is driest just east of the lee sides of the mountains. A prime example is the White Mountains in California. This 14,000-foot range is just as high as the Sierra Nevada just across the Owens Valley to the west, but it is far drier. As the moisture-starved air descends in the lee of the mountains, it warms rapidly (5.5 degrees per 1,000 feet), which lowers the humidity even further and greatly increases the drying power of the air. This is the beginning of the Great Basin Desert, which covers all of Nevada except the southern tip. The Mohave Desert covers the southern tip of Nevada, southeastern California, and a bit of northwestern Arizona and southwestern Utah.

It's hard to believe that this faint track through the desert was once the main highway between Salt Lake City and Los Angeles. There were no hotels or motels along most of the route, so early motorists camped along the way.

ARROWHEAD ROAD

The Arrowhead Road was one of the first roads through this area and was the main route for motorists traveling from Salt Lake City to Las Vegas and Los Angeles, decades before the first paved highways were built along the present route of I-15. Built in 1914 and used until 1929, travelers had very few amenities, and most camped along the way. Breakdowns were frequent, so most people traveled in small convoys of two or more cars. Although drivers were lucky to hit 25 miles per hour, it was speedy and luxurious travel compared to the stagecoaches that cars were rapidly replacing.

Arrowhead Trail

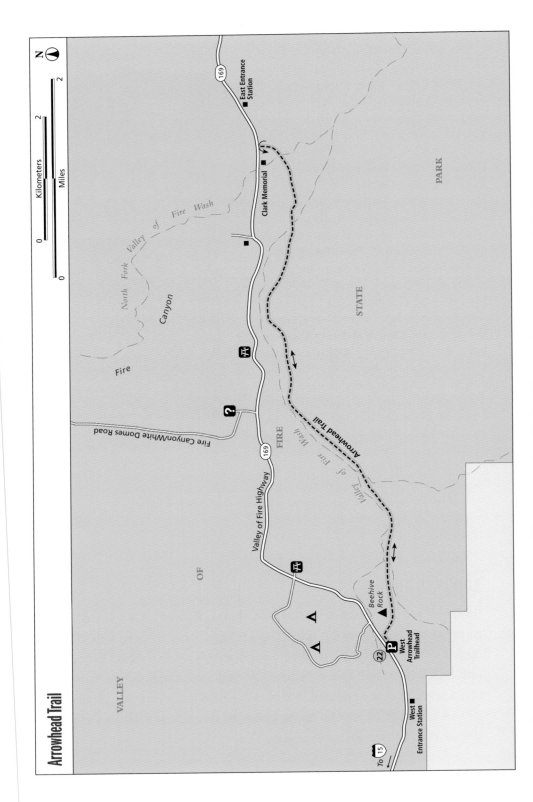

Another cause of deserts is remoteness from large moisture sources. The Valley of Fire and southern Nevada are not only far from the Pacific Ocean, they are also distant from the Atlantic at the Gulf of Mexico, which is the main source of summer moisture. As the North American monsoon develops in late summer, a gentle flow of moist air moves northwest from the Gulf of Mexico and triggers afternoon thunderstorms. These storms are most intense in Mexico, west Texas, and New Mexico, and become less intense further northwest. The North American monsoon is the reason that the Sonoran Desert of southern Arizona and northwestern Mexico is the wettest and lushest of the four American deserts.

A more general cause of desert formation is latitude. It is no coincidence that the major deserts of the world are centered on the Tropics of Cancer and Capricorn. The majority of the world's deserts occur along the Tropic of Cancer in the Northern Hemisphere because the Northern Hemisphere has more land than the Southern Hemisphere. The North American deserts and the Sahara, Arabian, Indian, Iranian, Kara-Kum, Kyzyl-Kum, Taklimakan, and Gobi Deserts all occur near the Tropic of Cancer. In the Southern Hemisphere, deserts along the Tropic of Capricorn include the Australian, the Kalahari, Namib, the Atacama-Peruvian, and the Patagonian.

These two desert belts occur where they do because of the general global air circulation. Air is heated at the equator, ascends, loses much of its moisture as rain over the tropics, and then moves toward the poles. It descends and heats up in the high-pressure zones centered over the Tropics of Cancer and Capricorn. In the temperate latitudes the air once again ascends, producing higher precipitation. Finally, in the polar regions, the air descends again, creating polar regions of low precipitation (the polar regions have a lot of snow and ice not because of heavy snowfall, but because there is no melting most of the year).

Miles and Directions

0.0   Hike east from the West Arrowhead Trailhead following the obvious old road.

0.4   Follow the trail around the south side of Beehive Rock.

1.4   Pass through a 0.25-mile-wide gap between rock formations, where the Arrowhead Trail turns northeast.

3.0   The trail turns east, at a point directly south of the visitor center.

4.9   Arrowhead Trail leaves Valley of Fire Wash and heads northeast.

6.0   The trail ends at Valley of Fire Highway. Return the way you came.

12.0   Arrive back at the West Arrowhead Trailhead.

23 Elephant Rock Loop

This loop hike follows a portion of the historic Arrowhead Road and leads past odd rock formations.

Start: 54.1 miles northeast of Las Vegas
Distance: 1.3-mile loop with a short cherry stem
Approximate hiking time: 1 hour
Difficulty: Easy due to little elevation change
Trail surface: Dirt and rocks, sand, old road
Best seasons: Fall through spring
Water: None
Other trail users: None
Canine compatibility: Leashed dogs permitted, maximum 6-foot leash

Fees and permits: Entrance fee
Schedule: Open all hours
Maps: CalTopo.com MapBuilder Topo layer; USGS Valley of Fire East
Trail contacts: Valley of Fire State Park, 29450 Valley of Fire Rd., Overton 89040; (702) 397-2088; http://parks.nv.gov/parks/valley-of-fire
Special considerations: During the summer hike early in the day and carry plenty of water.

Finding the trailhead: From the intersection of US 95 and I-15 in downtown Las Vegas, drive 32.8 miles north on I-15. Turn right on the Valley of Fire Highway and drive 21.3 miles to the Elephant Rock Trailhead, just before leaving Valley of Fire State Park at the east entrance. GPS: N36 25.675'/W114 27.644'

The Hike

From the Elephant Rock Trailhead, follow the Elephant Rock Trail west toward the red rock formations next to the highway. Stay left at the junction with the Arrowhead Trail to start the loop. The Elephant Rock Trail turns southwest and passes between Elephant Rock and the highway, then parallels the highway until it comes out into more open terrain. The trail then turns northwest and crosses a small bridge. Just across the bridge the trail meets the Arrowhead Trail, where you'll turn right to follow it to the north. As the trail approaches the base of the bluffs to the north, it turns right (east) and heads toward a pass north of Elephant Rock. After crossing the pass, where sections of the old auto road are badly eroded, the trail rounds the north side of Elephant Rock. Turn left at the trail junction to return to the Elephant Rock Trailhead.

The night sky is spectacular on a clear night from Valley of Fire, which is far enough from the lights of Las Vegas to keep the sky from being washed out. If you're camping during the winter or spring, walk away from the campground lights in the evening and look for the following constellations. A star chart or a phone app such as Cosmic Watch or Sky Map will show the sky at the date and time you're observing it, and help you get oriented.

This bridge was used in the movie Star Trek: Generations *to film the scene in which Captain James T. Kirk meets his end.*

To the north, look low on the horizon for Ursa Major, the Great Bear, which looks like a large dipper with the bowl to the right and the handle parallel to the ground. In the spring Ursa Major will be farther to the east, standing on its handle. The Big Dipper, as the dipper part of the constellation is popularly known, is actually an asterism—a star formation that is part of one of the eighty-eight recognized constellations.

The two right-hand stars of the Big Dipper are the Pointer Stars. If you draw an imaginary line upward through the Pointer Stars, you'll come to a star of medium brightness, which is Polaris, the North Star. Polaris is the only star that doesn't appear to move as the earth turns, and always indicates the direction north. A smaller, fainter dipper, the Little Dipper, extends to the left of Polaris with its dipper upside down. The Little Dipper is part of the constellation Ursa Minor, the Little Bear. In the spring the Little Dipper hangs by its handle from Polaris.

▶ **The small steel bridge on this hike was used to film the scene in the movie *Star Trek: Generations* in which Captain James T. Kirk finally meets his end on the alien planet Veridian Three. Kirk was captain of the starship *Enterprise* in the original 1960s TV series, and his character appeared in several of the *Star Trek* movies.**

Up and to the right of Polaris is the constellation Cassiopeia, a group of bright stars that looks like an "M" tipped onto its right side (in the spring it will be above and slightly left of Polaris, and the "M" will be upright).

Elephant Rock Loop

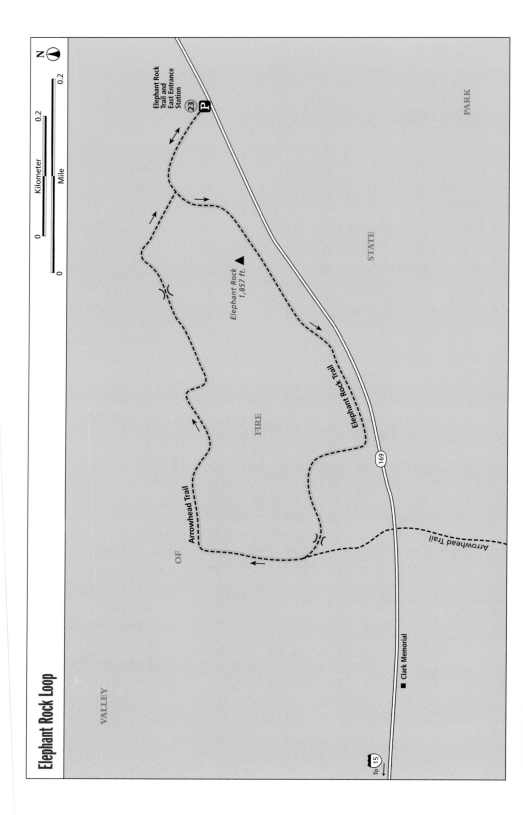

N

0   0.2   Kilometer   0.2

0   Mile

Elephant Rock Trail and East Entrance Station

P

(23)

Elephant Rock
1,857 ft. ▲

Arrowhead Trail

Elephant Rock Trail

Arrowhead Trail

(169)

VALLEY   OF   FIRE   STATE   PARK

■ Clark Memorial

To (15)

Look nearly overhead for the Great Square, a large square of bright stars that is part of the constellation Pegasus, the Winged Horse. A large curving V of stars uses one corner of the Great Square as its apex, the constellation Andromeda. If you have binoculars and it's a moonless night, look along the V for a faint fuzzy object, Andromeda Galaxy, the only galaxy outside our own Milky Way that is visible with the naked eye. In the spring Pegasus and Andromeda will be in the eastern sky.

During the winter look to the southeast for Orion the Hunter, which is one of the most prominent constellations in the winter sky. Four bright stars form a tall rectangle, and the star at the upper left is distinctly reddish in color. This is the giant red star Betelgeuse, which is many times larger than our own sun. Three bright stars in a row across the middle of the rectangle are the Hunter's belt, and a smaller line of bright stars below it are his sword.

Miles and Directions

0.0   From the Elephant Rock Trailhead, hike west on the Elephant Rock Trail.

0.1   Turn left on the Elephant Rock Trail at a junction to start the loop in a clockwise direction.

0.5   The trail turns north away from the highway.

0.6   Cross a small steel bridge to join the Arrowhead Trail and turn right.

0.9   Cross the pass north of Elephant Rock.

1.2   At the trail junction, turn left to return to the trailhead.

1.3   Arrive back at the Elephant Rock Trailhead.

Red Rock Canyon

Although the upper half of the striking red and white sandstone cliffs at the southern end of the Spring Mountains is visible from west-facing hotel rooms in the towers along the Strip, most visitors to Las Vegas have no idea that such an outdoor destination exists only a few miles west of the casinos. Rather than a single canyon, Red Rock Canyon is actually a whole series of canyons cut deep into the 3,000-foot red and white sandstone cliffs that form an east-facing escarpment, formally named Sandstone Bluffs but referred to locally as the Red Rock Escarpment. Some of the canyons have permanent springs and seasonal creeks, and there are seasonal waterfalls as well. Trails range from very easy nature trails to challenging climbs of peaks and intricate treks across bare slickrock domes. Red Rock Canyon is also a well-known rock-climbing area, and climbers come from all

Multicolored sandstone cliffs rise thousands of feet above the mouth of Pine Creek Canyon. The color of the sandstone is caused by trace amounts of minerals such as iron oxide and reflects the environment in which the rocks were deposited.

in the valleys. Today salt flats and playas are the dried-out remains of those ancient lakes.

Along with the ubiquitous creosote bush, the Mohave Desert's other iconic plant is the Joshua tree. Although it doesn't grow in all of the Mohave Desert, it is found in the desert valleys at Red Rock Canyon. The Joshua tree is a tree-size yucca and is a member of the lily family. It grows up to 30 feet tall in favored locations, such as Joshua Tree National Park. At Red Rock Canyon it is smaller, reaching about 10 feet in height. Unfortunately, large wildfires, fueled by the exotic cheatgrass, have burned much of the desert plain below the Red Rock Escarpment and have killed many of the Joshua trees.

The Joshua tree certainly doesn't resemble most people's idea of a tree. The early explorer John C. Frémont regarded it as utterly repulsive. Joshua trees normally have a single trunk that branches a short distance above the ground. The ends of the branches are covered with a cluster of leaves and, when blooming, a mass of greenish to cream-colored flowers. The flowers are not fragrant. As more branches grow, Joshua trees begin to look treelike. Roots extend mostly horizontally from the base of the plant, and new plants may start from the root system.

Like all yuccas, Joshua trees are pollinated by moths and are dependent on them for propagation. When Joshua tree flowers blossom, female moths visit the flowers, gathering pollen and laying their eggs. The eggs hatch and the larvae feed on some of the seeds of the Joshua tree. Eventually the larvae fall to the ground, burrow in, and remain there until they become adult moths. The action of the female moth carrying pollen from plant to plant ensures the fertilization of the Joshua tree and ensures it will produce seeds for her young.

Miles and Directions

0.0 From the visitor center parking lot, hike southwest on the Moenkopi Loop.

0.1 The trail joins an old road now used as a trail, and turns right.

0.5 The Moenkopi Trail leaves the old road to the right and starts climbing along the south slopes of a low hill.

1.0 Follow a couple of switchbacks up the west side of the hill.

1.2 Reach the top of the hill and the high point of the hike. Continue north on the Moenkopi Trail as it descends a ridge.

1.5 The trail leaves the ridge and turns southeast back toward the visitor center, visible ahead. There are several unsigned hiker trails that lead north toward the Moenkopi Hills; stay right at each junction and keep heading toward the visitor center.

2.2 Arrive back at the visitor center.

GREEN TIP:
Before you start for home, have you left the wilderness as you'd want to see it?

25 Calico Hills

The Calico Hills are named for the contrasting bands of red and white sandstone that make up the slickrock domes and cliffs just north of the start of the scenic drive. This trail runs along a wash at the base of the Calico Hills between two scenic viewpoints on the scenic drive, and it provides access to the slickrock formations. This is a great hike for families, as children are fascinated by the rock formations.

Start: 18.7 miles west of Las Vegas
Distance: 1.4 miles out and back
Approximate hiking time: 2 hours
Difficulty: Easy due to little elevation change
Trail surface: Dirt, rocks, slickrock
Best season: All year
Water: None
Other trail users: None
Canine compatibility: Leashed dogs permitted
Fees and permits: Entrance fee
Schedule: Access is via the Scenic Drive, which is open daily Nov 1–Feb 28/29, 6 a.m.–5 p.m.; Mar 1–Mar 31, 7 a.m.–7 p.m.; Apr 1–Sept 30, 6 a.m.–8 p.m.; Oct 1–Oct 31, 6 a.m.–7 p.m.
Maps: CalTopo.com MapBuilder Topo layer; USGS La Madre Mountain
Trail contacts: Bureau of Land Management, Red Rock/Sloan Canyon Field Office, 1000 Scenic Loop Dr., Las Vegas 89161; (702) 515-5350; https://www.blm.gov/visit/red-rock-canyon-national-conservation-area
Special considerations: During the summer hike early in the day and carry plenty of water.

Finding the trailhead: From the intersection of US 95 and I-15 in downtown Las Vegas, drive 5.1 miles west on US 95. Exit onto Summerlin Parkway and drive 3.8 miles west. Exit onto Town Center Drive and turn left. Continue 2.3 miles, and then turn right onto West Charleston Boulevard, NV 159. Continue 6.2 miles, and then turn right (north) on the Red Rock Canyon Scenic Drive. Drive 1.2 miles to the Calico Hills 1 Viewpoint and Trailhead, on the right. GPS: N36 8.759'/W115 25.856'

The Hike

From the parking area, the trail drops a short distance down a ridge, and then turns left along the base of the slope below the road. It follows the unnamed wash northeast along the base of the Calico Hills, and then climbs a short distance up to the Calico Hills 2 Viewpoint and Trailhead. From here, return the way you came. There are many informal trails made by hikers and climbers that lead up into the Calico Hills, so you can spend quite a bit of time exploring. This is a popular rock-climbing area, and you will likely see several groups of rock climbers challenging their skills on the sandstone cliffs, especially on weekends.

The Aztec Sandstone that forms the Calico Hills and the Red Rock Escarpment across the valley is a deep and widespread layer of sandstone. It also covers large areas of far northern Arizona and southern Utah, where it is known as the Navajo Sandstone. Both Aztec and Navajo Sandstone are wind-deposited rock formations that

RAPPELLING AND ROCK CLIMBING SAFETY

Non-climbers often think the most exciting thing about rock climbing is rappelling, the technique of descending by sliding down a rope. Although rappelling is certainly exciting the first time you try it—the sensation of defying gravity is at once scary and exhilarating—the novelty soon wears off and the inherent dangers become apparent.

While actually climbing rock faces, climbers have at least three independent systems of protection that must fail before they can fall and get hurt. The first is the climber's skill in climbing the rock using natural holds. The second is the climbing rope, held by the climber's partner, and third, the anchors used to attach the rope to the rock. When rappelling, on the other hand, a climber is totally dependent on the anchor holding the rope at the top and the braking system used to control the descent. If either of these fails, the climber falls.

A surprising number of famous climbers have been killed while rappelling, so experienced climbers prefer to climb down or descend by an alternate route whenever possible.

once formed a vast erg, or Sahara-like desert. As you hike along the base of the Calico Hills, look closely at the sandstone. You'll see sloping layers in the rock. These are the slopes and slip faces of ancient sand dunes from the early Jurassic geologic period—the beginning of the age of the dinosaurs, about 200 million years ago.

At the base of the Aztec Sandstone in the Valley of Fire area, the rock layers show that the dune field was preceded by a desert plain drained by dry washes. The rocks from this period are mudstone and sandstone that was deposited by water, probably from seasonal floods. The desert contained seasonal water bodies that were drying out to become playas. The sand desert arrived in the form of small dunes and sheets of windblown sand. As more sand encroached on what is now southern Nevada, the dry washes and playas were buried under massive sand dunes.

The present Red Rock Canyon area was the western margin of this sea of sand, as evidenced by thin tongues of volcanic sediment that are present in the Aztec Sandstone. These layers of sediment probably represent the eastern margin

Rock climbers find plenty of challenging routes on the sandstone walls of the Calico Hills.

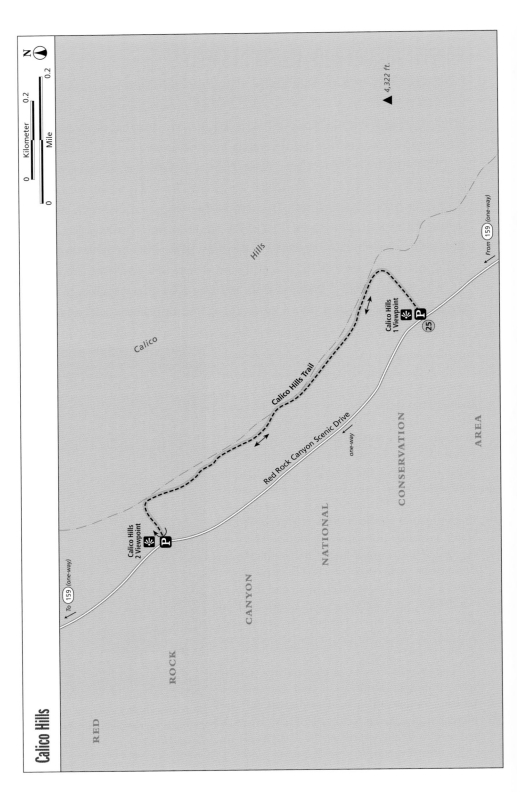

Calico Hills

N

0   Kilometer   0.2

0   Mile   0.2

RED

ROCK

CANYON

NATIONAL

CONSERVATION

AREA

Calico

Hills

4,322 ft.

Calico Hills Trail

Red Rock Canyon Scenic Drive

one-way

To 159 (one-way)

From 159 (one-way)

Calico Hills 2 Viewpoint

P

Calico Hills 1 Viewpoint

P

25

of an alluvial fan, or outwash plain, similar to those found at the foot of Nevada mountain ranges today.

To the south, in eastern California, volcanic rocks such as lava flows, tuff rocks derived from ash flows, debris flows, and outwash deposits show that the ancient sand desert encroached on an area of volcanoes. It would have been quite a landscape, where black volcanoes spewed ash and lava that partially covered a salmon-colored sea of sand.

In the end the erg, or sand desert, may have migrated completely across the region. While geological evidence in the Red Rock Canyon and Valley of Fire areas show the encroachment of the sand dunes, other evidence, far to the northeast in northern Utah and Wyoming, show the trailing edge of the sand desert.

Ultimately the sand desert was buried under thousands of feet of additional rock, and compression and heating formed the sandstone exposed today at the Calico Hills. A common question is why the Aztec Sandstone has alternating layers of white and salmon-colored rock. (The Calico Hills get their name from these alternating layers.) Apparently, iron oxide migrated through the sediments after they were buried by later rocks. Groundwater moving through the sediments bleached some areas and carried the iron oxides to others. Bleached areas of sandstone are white or light-colored, while areas containing iron oxides are reddish in color. Large-scale water movement was controlled by contacts between different layers of rock and by fault zones. Small-scale variations in color were caused by joints and local faults.

Miles and Directions

0.0 Leave the Calico Hills 1 Viewpoint and Trailhead by descending the trail to the northeast.

0.1 Turn left and follow the trail next to the wash along the base of the Calico Hills.

0.6 Turn left and follow the trail up to the scenic drive.

0.7 Arrive at Calico Hills 2 Viewpoint and Trailhead. Return the way you came.

1.4 Arrive back at the Calico Hills 1 Viewpoint and Trailhead.

26 Calico Tanks

This is an easy day hike to natural water tanks in the red rock Calico Hills. Such water tanks are vital for wildlife, and they were also important for natives and settlers.

Start: 20.2 miles west of Las Vegas
Distance: 2.0 miles out and back
Approximate hiking time: 1 hour
Difficulty: Easy due to minor elevation change
Trail surface: Dirt and rocks
Best season: All year
Water: None
Other trail users: None
Canine compatibility: Leashed dogs permitted
Fees and permits: Entrance fee
Schedule: Access is via the Scenic Drive, which is open daily Nov 1–Feb 28/29, 6 a.m.–5 p.m.; Mar 1–Mar 31, 7 a.m.–7 p.m.; Apr 1–Sept 30, 6 a.m.–8 p.m.; Oct 1–Oct 31, 6 a.m.–7 p.m.
Maps: CalTopo.com MapBuilder Topo layer; USGS La Madre Mountain
Trail contacts: Bureau of Land Management, Red Rock/Sloan Canyon Field Office, 1000 Scenic Loop Dr., Las Vegas 89161; (702) 515-5350; https://www.blm.gov/visit/red-rock-canyon-national-conservation-area
Special considerations: During the summer hike early in the day and carry plenty of water.

Finding the trailhead: From the intersection of US 95 and I-15 in downtown Las Vegas, drive 5.1 miles west on US 95. Exit onto Summerlin Parkway and drive 3.8 miles west. Exit onto Town Center Drive and turn left. Continue 2.3 miles, and then turn right onto West Charleston Boulevard, NV 159. Continue 6.2 miles, and then turn right (north) on the Red Rock Canyon Scenic Drive. Drive 2.8 miles to the Calico Hills 1 Viewpoint and Trailhead, on the right. GPS: N36 9.718'/W115 27.008'

The Hike

Follow the wash north 0.25 mile, then turn right (east) at the third canyon and continue up a side canyon through the red slickrock to a large natural water tank (tinaja). When they have water, this and other tinajas in the Calico Hills are important sources of water for the area's wildlife.

Animals have many other survival strategies to help them cope with the heat and dryness of the desert. Many desert animals are nocturnal, at least in the summer. They avoid the extreme heat of day by nesting or denning up until the coolness and higher humidity of evening set in. Burrowing animals have a major advantage in that their occupied burrows are at about 80 degrees Fahrenheit year-round, and the humidity remains at a comfortably high level due to ground moisture and moisture given off by the animal. On the desert surface, summer humidity often drops to just a few percent during the day, which quickly dehydrates any animal without a source of water. Many birds stay in their nests in trees, where the temperature is 10 or 20 degrees cooler than that near the ground. Soaring birds climb to great heights with little expenditure of energy, rising on the strong updrafts created by the sun beating on expanses of bare rock and open areas. Since the temperature of dry air falls at 5.5 degrees Fahrenheit for every 1,000 feet of elevation gained, those buzzards, ravens, and hawks that are tiny specks high in the summer sky really are laughing at you—they are sailing around in cool air while you fry in the ground heat.

Animals such as desert bighorn sheep can go days without water, but eventually they do need a drink. Others, such as the kangaroo rat, never drink liquid water. They extract all the water they need from their food.

Insects and spiders would be quickly broiled by the extreme desert heat found within a few inches of the ground, which often exceeds 150 degrees Fahrenheit during the day. Some insects, such as ants, take advantage of burrows during summer days, while in the winter they forage in broad daylight, taking advantage of the ground warmed to a comfortable temperature by the winter sun. Other insects and spiders use the

Calico Tanks hold water from storm runoff and are an essential water source for wildlife. Desert hikers should never swim or bathe in such natural water tanks because they are easily polluted.

cool and moist microclimates found under rocks, logs, and bark. The common bark

SLICKROCK

The origin and exact meaning of the term "slickrock" is unclear. It is generally used in the American Southwest to describe areas of exposed sandstone such as the Calico Hills. In arid climates sandstone often erodes to form sleekly rounded domes and turrets. From a distance the term is descriptive, but up close, the hiker will discover that the rock is anything but slick. It is nature's sandpaper, composed of billions of grains of sand cemented together by heat and pressure. Contrary to popular opinion, slickrock country is primarily eroded by water during occasional desert storms. Wind plays a very minor role.

Calico Tanks

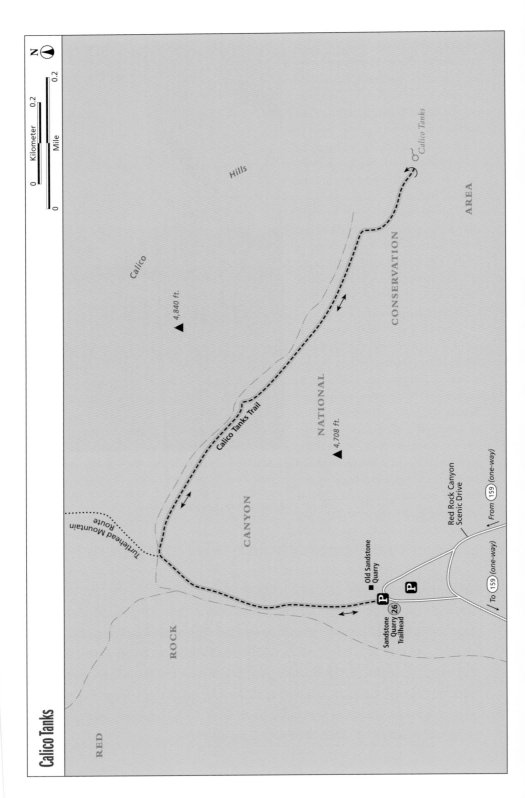

N

0 0.2 Kilometer
0 0.2 Mile

Calico Tanks

CONSERVATION

AREA

Hills

Calico

4,840 ft.

Calico Tanks Trail

NATIONAL

4,708 ft.

Turtlehead Mountain Route

CANYON

Old Sandstone Quarry

ROCK

RED

Sandstone Quarry Trailhead 26

P

P

Red Rock Canyon Scenic Drive

From 159 (one-way)

To 159 (one-way)

depiction on the topo. You can also choose easier routes of travel and locate the best campsites.

A GPS receiver is useful but not essential. Never depend on a GPS unit alone for backcountry navigation. The batteries can run down, the unit can fail, and you may be in a place where the unit can't pick up enough satellites to navigate. If you do carry a GPS, learn how to use it before you take it on a hike.

There are numerous cell phone mapping apps that take advantage of the GPS receivers built into all phones to provide trail maps. While the best of these are very useful (for the Las Vegas area, I recommend CalTopo and Gaia GPS), cell phones have notoriously short battery life. I always carry a printed map when hiking off-trail.

As you hike, keep track of your location by noting trail junctions and landmarks such as wash or stream crossings, peaks, saddles, and other distinctive features. Also look back to see what the landscape will look like on your return. At rest stops, or more often in complex country, get out your map and note your location. On long hikes through difficult terrain, you might want to note the time as well as the place by writing it on the map. As you hike, you'll get an idea of your rate of progress and whether you'll make it to the trailhead or camp by dark.

By lunchtime, or halfway through the time you've allotted for the hike, you should be at your destination on an out-and-back hike or halfway on a loop or shuttle hike. If not, turn back to avoid being late or caught in the dark.

Miles and Directions

0.0 From the Sandstone Quarry Trailhead, start on the Calico Tanks Trail.

0.3 Leave the Calico Tanks Trail and hike north up the wash.

1.2 Enter the ravine west of Turtlehead Mountain.

1.6 At the head of the ravine, turn right and hike southeast to the summit.

2.0 Arrive at Turtlehead Mountain. Return the way you came.

4.0 Arrive back at the Sandstone Quarry Trailhead.

28 Keystone Thrust

This is an easy day hike to a unique geologic feature, the Keystone Thrust fault. This contact zone is a place where older rocks have been overturned and thrust on top of younger rocks.

Start: 23.8 miles west of Las Vegas
Distance: 1.6 miles out and back
Approximate hiking time: 1 hour
Difficulty: Easy due to no elevation change
Trail surface: Dirt and rocks
Best season: All year
Water: None
Other trail users: None
Canine compatibility: Leashed dogs permitted
Fees and permits: Entrance fee
Schedule: Access is via the Scenic Drive, which is open daily Nov 1–Feb 28/29, 6 a.m.–5 p.m.;

Mar 1–Mar 31, 7 a.m.–7 p.m.; Apr 1–Sept 30, 6 a.m.–8 p.m.; Oct 1–Oct 31, 6 a.m.–7 p.m.
Maps: CalTopo.com MapBuilder Topo layer; USGS La Madre Mountain
Trail contacts: Bureau of Land Management, Red Rock/Sloan Canyon Field Office, 1000 Scenic Loop Dr., Las Vegas 89161; (702) 515-5350; https://www.blm.gov/visit/red-rock-canyon-national-conservation-area
Special considerations: During the summer hike early in the day and carry plenty of water.

Finding the trailhead: From the intersection of US 95 and I-15 in downtown Las Vegas, drive 5.1 miles west on US 95. Exit onto Summerlin Parkway and drive 3.8 miles west. Exit onto Town Center Drive and turn left. Continue 2.3 miles, and then turn right onto West Charleston Boulevard, NV 159. Continue 6.2 miles, and then turn right (north) on the Red Rock Canyon Scenic Drive. Drive 5.9 miles, then turn right into a gravel road. Drive 0.5 mile to the end of the road at the White Rock Spring Trailhead. GPS: N36 10.396'/W115 28.638'

The Hike

Start on the Keystone Thrust Trail on the right side of the parking area. The trail descends into and crosses a wash, then climbs north up the slope. Next, the trail climbs northeast into a small saddle. Just up the ridge the trail forks, with the right fork descending off the ridge into a small canyon. The contact of the Keystone Thrust fault is visible below, where the older gray limestone has been forced over the top of the much younger red and white Aztec Sandstone.

In geology a fault is a fracture along a plane in the rock where the rocks on one side of the fault are displaced in relation to the other side. A dip–slip fault is one where the movement (slip) on the fault is nearly vertical. If the slip along the fault is approximately horizontal, the fault is termed a strike-slip fault. A fault with a combination of both vertical and horizontal movement is an oblique-slip fault. A fault line is the line where a fault meets the earth's surface. Most faults consist of more than one parallel fracture, so they are referred to as fault zones.

The Keystone Thrust fault resulted in the older gray limestone, at the top of the photo, being pushed horizontally over the top of the younger, salmon-colored sandstone at the bottom of the photo, upsetting the expectation that younger rocks are always found on top of older rocks.

Large-scale faults are caused by tectonic forces created by the movement of the continental and oceanic plates. The famous San Andreas Fault in western California is the point of collision between the Pacific and North American Plates. The San Andreas is actually a fault zone consisting of many parallel faults. Earthquakes commonly take place along large faults. Small-scale faults occur from local movement such as the settling of an isolated butte separated from the main mass of rock by erosion.

Rocks cannot just slip easily past each other. Because of friction and the solidity of the rock, the relative motion causes stress to build up. When the stress builds up to a critical point, the rock moves suddenly and releases the stored potential energy as an earthquake. Such earthquakes can occur along a fault near the earth's surface, or deep within the earth on faults that are not visible at the surface.

As the rocks move past each other along a fault, the friction and heating creates a zone where the rocks have been modified, known as fault rock. Typically, the fault rock consists of a fine-grained matrix of sharp fragments and larger embedded pieces of broken-off rock, but fine or glassy rock may be present in some fault zones.

In a normal, sloping dip-slip fault, the earth's crust is being extended and the rock on the top of the sloping fault slides down and away from the other layer. In a reverse fault the earth's crust is being compressed and the rock on top of the sloping fault rides over the rock on the lower side of the fault.

A thrust fault is a form of reverse fault where the fault is nearly parallel to the earth's surface and one rock layer is thrust horizontally over another. Normally younger rocks are found on top of older rocks, as they are deposited in layered succession over time. But here the older limestone has been pushed over the top of the

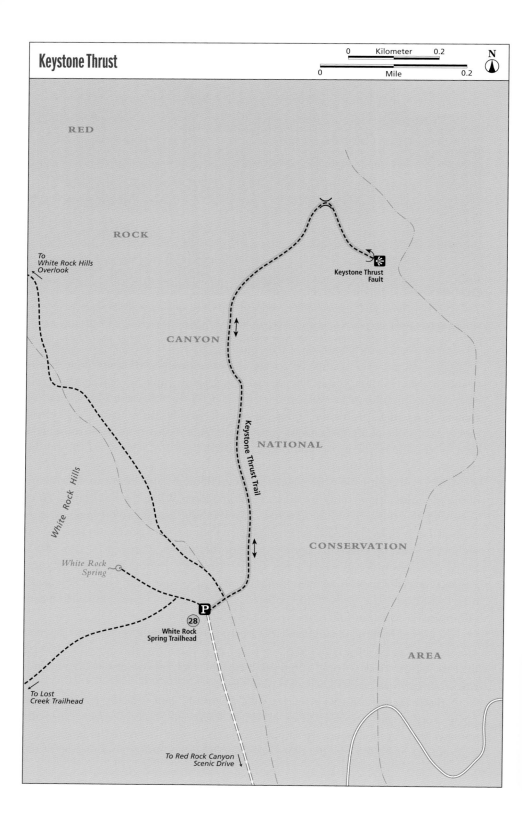

Keystone Thrust

0 — Kilometer — 0.2

0 — Mile — 0.2

N

RED

ROCK

To
White Rock Hills
Overlook

Keystone Thrust
Fault

CANYON

NATIONAL

Keystone Thrust Trail

White Rock Hills

White Rock
Spring

CONSERVATION

P

28

White Rock
Spring Trailhead

To Lost
Creek Trailhead

AREA

To Red Rock Canyon
Scenic Drive

younger sandstone. It is believed that this occurred about sixty-five million years ago when two continental plates collided to create the present North American continent. The thrust contact is clearly defined by the sharp contrast between the gray limestone and the red sandstone. The Keystone Thrust fault extends from the Cottonwood Fault (along the Pahrump Highway) 13.0 miles northward to the vicinity of La Madre Mountain, where it is obscured by more complex faulting. Thrust faults are common in mountainous regions because of the violence of the forces that created the mountains, but the Keystone Thrust fault is one of the best exposed in the world.

In some mountain regions, such as the Alps, multiple thrust faults created very complex layering in the rock. Later erosion removed much of the original rock, making the thrust faults much less obvious, and confusing the relationships between rocks. Early geologists found such thrust fault regions difficult to decipher.

Miles and Directions

0.0 Leave the White Rock Spring Trailhead on the Keystone Thrust Trail. At about 250 feet, a faint hiker trail goes off to the left (northwest) to the White Rock Hills Overlook.

0.7 At the saddle, turn right and descend into a small canyon.

0.8 Arrive at Keystone Thrust. Return the way you came.

1.6 Arrive back at the White Rock Spring Trailhead.

29 White Rock Hills Overlook

Enjoy an easy day hike on an informal trail to a vantage point that features a dramatic view of the valley between the White Rock Hills and La Madre Mountain.

Start: 23.8 miles west of Las Vegas
Distance: 2.6 miles out and back
Approximate hiking time: 2 hours
Difficulty: Easy due to little elevation change
Trail surface: Dirt and rocks
Best season: All year
Water: None
Other trail users: None
Canine compatibility: Leashed dogs permitted
Fees and permits: Entrance fee
Schedule: Access is via the Scenic Drive, which is open daily Nov 1–Feb 28/29, 6 a.m.–5 p.m.;

Mar 1–Mar 31, 7 a.m.–7 p.m.; Apr 1–Sept 30, 6 a.m.–8 p.m.; Oct 1–Oct 31, 6 a.m.–7 p.m.
Maps: CalTopo.com MapBuilder Topo layer; USGS La Madre Spring, La Madre Mountain
Trail contacts: Bureau of Land Management, Red Rock/Sloan Canyon Field Office, 1000 Scenic Loop Dr., Las Vegas 89161; (702) 515-5350; https://www.blm.gov/visit/red-rock-canyon-national-conservation-area
Special considerations: During the summer hike early in the day and carry plenty of water.

Finding the trailhead: From the intersection of US 95 and I-15 in downtown Las Vegas, drive 5.1 miles west on US 95. Exit onto Summerlin Parkway and drive 3.8 miles west. Exit onto Town Center Drive and turn left. Continue 2.3 miles, and then turn right onto West Charleston Boulevard, NV 159. Continue 6.2 miles, and then turn right (north) on the Red Rock Canyon Scenic Drive. Drive 5.9 miles, then turn right into a gravel road. Drive 0.5 mile to the end of the road at the White Rock Spring Trailhead. GPS: N36 10.396'/W115 28.638'

The Hike

Start the hike on the Keystone Thrust Trail, which leaves the right side of the parking area and drops into a wash. Leave the trail on the left and continue up the wash along the base of the sandstone bluffs. After about 0.5 mile follow an informal trail that veers out of the wash to the right. A few cairns mark the route as it parallels the wash. Soon the trail reaches a saddle with excellent views of the west side of the White Rock Hills and the valley below La Madre Mountain. The towering limestone cliffs of La Madre Mountain to the north make a somber contrast with the bright sandstone to the left.

Like the other trails and vantage points near the White Rock Hills, this trail and viewpoint are good places to watch for bighorn sheep. About the size of a small deer, desert bighorn sheep average about 4 feet long and weigh between 100 and 200

GREEN TIP:
Pack out your dog's waste or dispose of it in a trashcan or a hole dug into the ground.

pounds. They are grayish-tan in color in order to better blend into their desert surroundings. Mature males have massive horns that spiral backward then forward to a nearly complete circle. Female bighorns have much smaller horns that usually form less than a semicircle. Neither the male nor the female ever shed their horns.

Desert bighorn sheep apparently had a much larger range before modern man took over much of the landscape. They require solitude and now are confined to remote desert mountain ranges. In some areas the desert bighorn are classified as an endangered species. Hunting is strictly controlled, but poaching by trophy hunters takes a toll.

Bighorn sheep are well adapted to desert life, but they do need water every few days in hot weather and less often in cool weather. They travel in small family groups of about

The White Rock Hills are named for the light-colored sandstone composing the hills, which stands in sharp contrast to the gray limestone of the nearby La Madre Mountains.

three to five animals and tend to favor steep, rocky hillsides where they can look down on any approaching threats. If disturbed, the band will move higher up the mountainside, so the best tactic for spotting them is to stop for an extended period, listen, and scan the hillsides above you. Binoculars are a help.

Another desert adaptation is the bighorn sheep's manner of grazing on desert vegetation. They rarely eat entire plants, allowing the slow-growing plants to survive and regenerate. The small bands of sheep have less impact on their environment than

▶ Juniper trees commonly grow in association with piñon pines, forming a forest community called piñon-juniper woodland, or PJ for short. Piñon pines tend to favor slightly higher and cooler slopes, while junipers favor slightly lower and warmer slopes. The bluish juniper berries are an important food for wildlife. The slopes of the White Rock Hills above the trail are a good example of piñon-juniper woodland.

White Rock Hills Overlook

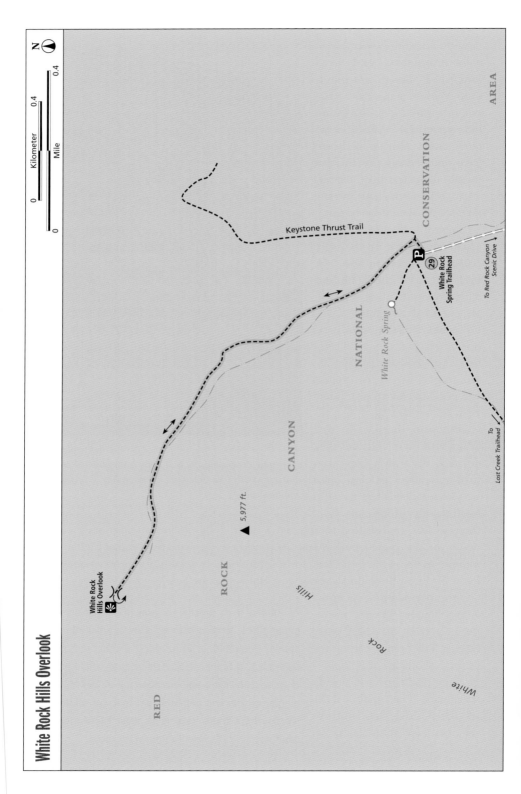

White Rock Hills Overlook

RED

ROCK

HILLS

Rock

White

5,977 ft.

CANYON

NATIONAL

White Rock Spring

CONSERVATION

AREA

Keystone Thrust Trail

P

29

White Rock
Spring Trailhead

To Red Rock Canyon
Scenic Drive

To
Lost Creek Trailhead

N

Kilometer
0   0.4

Mile
0   0.4

animals that travel in large herds. Bighorn sheep can live for long periods on dead or dormant plants, but they do eat green forage when it is available, which supplies part of the animal's water and reduces the need to travel to water sources.

Although bighorn sheep are preyed on by mountain lions, coyotes, bobcats, and golden eagles, their main predator is man. The human effect is mainly to reduce sheep habitat by hunting, mining, taking water sources and rangelands for domestic livestock, introduction of wild burros and disease, housing developments, and highways. Highways are a major problem for the sheep because they will not cross busy roads, and the effect is to isolate the populations in adjacent mountain ranges from each other.

▶ The Keystone Thrust fault is responsible for the fact that the younger sandstones of the White Rock Hills are found below the older limestone layers. The younger, brighter layers of Aztec Sandstone even look younger than the gray limestones.

Wild burros are also a major threat to the desert bighorn sheep because they aggressively compete for water and forage. They monopolize and foul water sources, discouraging the bighorn from drinking as often as they need. Burros also trample the vegetation around springs and water sources, destroying a valuable source of food for the sheep and other native animals. In some areas, such as Grand Canyon National Park, land managers have removed all or most of the wild burro population to help the desert bighorn sheep population recover. In the Grand Canyon the program has been spectacularly effective. Hikers commonly see bighorn even from the trails, whereas before the burro reduction, it was rare to see the wild sheep even in really remote areas.

Miles and Directions

0.0 Leave the White Rock Spring Trailhead, and go west down an old dirt road. In about 250 feet leave this trail, turning left (to the northwest) on a faint, unmarked hiker trail.

0.5 Follow the trail as it veers out of the wash to the right.

1.3 Reach the saddle overlooking La Madre Spring valley. Return the way you came.

2.6 Arrive back at the White Rock Spring Trailhead.

30 Willow Spring Loop

This hike features a variety of plant communities including riparian, pines, oaks, and sagebrush desert. You can also see prehistoric pits that were used by natives to roast food.

Start: 25.5 miles west of Las Vegas
Distance: 1.0-mile loop
Approximate hiking time: 1 hour
Difficulty: Easy
Trail surface: Dirt and rocks, sand and gravel
Best season: All year
Water: None
Other trail users: None
Canine compatibility: Leashed dogs permitted
Fees and permits: Entrance fee
Schedule: Access is via the Scenic Drive, which is open daily Nov 1–Feb 28/29, 6 a.m.–5 p.m.; Mar 1–Mar 31, 7 a.m.–7 p.m.; Apr 1–Sept 30, 6 a.m.–8 p.m.; Oct 1–Oct 31, 6 a.m.–7 p.m.
Maps: CalTopo.com MapBuilder Topo layer; USGS La Madre Spring, La Madre Mountain
Trail contacts: Bureau of Land Management, Red Rock/Sloan Canyon Field Office, 1000 Scenic Loop Dr., Las Vegas 89161; (702) 515-5350; https://www.blm.gov/visit/red-rock-canyon-national-conservation-area
Special considerations: During the summer hike early in the day and carry plenty of water.

Finding the trailhead: From the intersection of US 95 and I-15 in downtown Las Vegas, drive 5.1 miles west on US 95. Exit onto Summerlin Parkway and drive 3.8 miles west. Exit onto Town Center Drive and turn left. Continue 2.3 miles, and then turn right onto West Charleston Boulevard, NV 159. Continue 6.2 miles, and then turn right (north) on the Red Rock Canyon Scenic Drive. Drive 7.1 miles, then turn right onto the Willow Spring Picnic Area road. Continue 0.9 mile to the Willow Spring Picnic Area, on the right. GPS: N36 9.611'/W115 29.879'

The Hike

From the Willow Spring Picnic Area, walk to the right and follow the Willow Spring Trail along the base of the White Rock Hills. You'll pass several Native American roasting pits (sometimes called mescal pits) and then cross the road to the Lost Creek parking area. Now, follow the right fork of the Lost Creek Trail across the wash. Turn right at a junction on the southwest side of the wash to stay on the Willow Spring Trail. After a short distance the trail turns right and crosses the wash to the Willow Spring Picnic Area.

Desert plants have several means of adapting to the dry, hot conditions of the desert. Regardless of the means, all plants need water—about 80 to 90 percent of most plant tissue is water. Water is required to support the chemical reactions that sustain the plant, including the vital process of photosynthesis (using sunlight to make food), and it provides a transport mechanism for minerals and other chemicals within the plant. Plant cells are full of water under slight pressure, which provides support for most plants. Transpiration of water from the leaves of plants cools the plant.

Native roasting pits such as this one were used by generations of Native Americans to roast foods such as agave roots.

Photosynthesis is essentially the basis of life, both plant and animal, and the process must go on even under harsh conditions, or life cannot exist in the desert. In photosynthesis, plants use sunlight, water, carbon dioxide, and chlorophyll to make complex carbohydrates, which the plants use as food. In turn, animals consume the plants and process their carbohydrates as food.

Plants absorb water through their roots and take in carbon dioxide through stomates, small pores in the leaves and stems. Oxygen is a waste product of photosynthesis and is vented through the same stomates. The challenge that desert plants face is how to continue this process while conserving limited water.

Plants that require a great deal of water do grow in the desert, but only in riparian zones along streams or near springs. Such plants include cottonwood trees, willows, and sycamore trees, which essentially escape the desert by living in the rare water-rich environments within the desert.

Another means of escaping the arid reality of the desert is by growing only during wet periods and spending dry periods as seeds. The spring flower show that the desert can put on after wet winters is composed of these plants. They are annuals, but

GREEN TIP:
Don't take souvenirs home with you. This means natural materials such as plants, rocks, shells, fossils, and wood as well as historic artifacts such as potsherds and arrowheads.

A VARIED NATIVE MENU

Ancient inhabitants slow-cooked agave plants, other vegetables, and meats in roasting pits. The food was placed in a bed of hot coals mixed with cobbles and covered with plant materials and earth. After enough time had passed, the cooked food, ash, and fire-cracked rock were dug out. The discarded rock and ash forms a doughnut-shaped ring often several feet high and containing thousands of heating rocks. The vast quantity of rocks shows how long some of these pits were in use. Also known as mescal pits, these cooking sites are common in the Southwest.

Another important food source for natives and wildlife alike is the singleleaf piñon pine. The singleleaf piñon is easily recognized since it is the only pine with needles growing singly, as the name implies, rather than in bunches of two or more. Like its cousin the Colorado piñon, the seeds are edible and used to be an important food source for the native inhabitants, who would gather in temporary villages in places where the pine nut harvest was good. Pine nuts are a human delicacy often used in Southwestern-style cooking and are still an important food source for birds and small mammals.

because the favorable period for their growth and propagation is so short, they complete their life cycle from seed to flowering plant to seed much faster than their counterparts in wet climates. A better term for these plants is ephemerals. They require more than just a wet winter to flower in the spring—soil temperature is important also. Looking at the desert floor in the summer, it's hard to believe that billions of seeds are waiting in the barren-looking soil for just the right conditions to transform the desert into a carpet of rich green and brightly colored flowers.

Yet another method desert plants use for survival is saving water. All cactus and a few other plants such as agave are water-saving plants. These plants have extensive but shallow root systems that are very efficient at gathering water after a rain. Many cactus can even sprout special rain roots to help collect moisture. They then store the water in their succulent flesh. Barrel and saguaro cactus both have accordion-like pleats in their skins that expand as the plant takes on water. The next trick is to save that water from loss through the skin. Most cactus have a waxy skin that prevents water loss when the stomates are closed during the heat of the day. Many cactus avoid daytime photosynthesis by a process that involves absorbing carbon dioxide by opening the stomata at night when it is cooler, and storing the carbon dioxide as an organic acid. During the day, when the stomates are closed, the cactus completes the process of photosynthesis with the organic acid. As a result of being so careful with water, most cactus are very slow growing.

Tolerators are a group of desert plants that employ several methods to survive heat and dryness. Many of these plants, such as mesquite, have very deep taproots that can

Willow Spring Loop

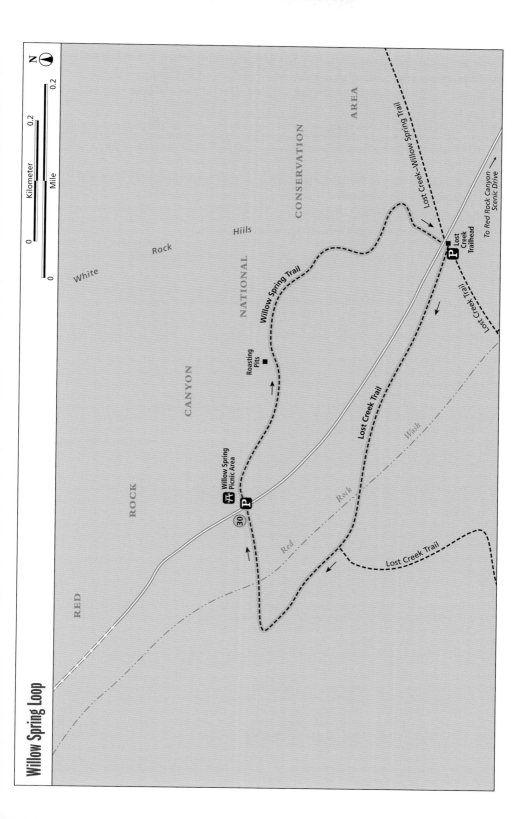

RED ROCK CANYON NATIONAL CONSERVATION AREA

White

Rock

Hiils

Red Rock

Wash

Willow Spring Picnic Area

Roasting Pits

Willow Spring Trail

Lost Creek Trail

Lost Creek Trail

Lost Creek Trail

Lost Creek–Willow Spring Trail

Lost Creek Trailhead

To Red Rock Canyon Scenic Drive

N

Kilometer

Mile

0   0.2

0   0.2

30

reach a reliable year-round water source. The root structure is usually much larger than the visible plant. For example, the paloverde tree of the Sonoran Desert usually grows about 10 to 15 feet high yet can send a taproot down 100 feet.

Miles and Directions

0.0   Leave Willow Spring Picnic Area on the Willow Spring Trail at the right side of the parking area.

0.5   Cross the highway to the Lost Creek Trailhead and then follow the right fork of the Lost Creek Trail across Rock Wash.

0.8   Turn right on the Willow Spring Trail.

1.0   Cross the road and arrive at Willow Spring Trailhead.

31 La Madre Spring

This hike provides a good wildlife-viewing opportunity. You may see bighorn sheep, deer, and other wildlife in the vicinity of La Madre Spring, which has been improved to provide a better source of water for wildlife.

Start: 25.7 miles west of Las Vegas
Distance: 3.8 miles out and back
Approximate hiking time: 2 hours
Difficulty: Easy
Trail surface: Dirt and rocks
Best season: All year
Water: None
Other trail users: None
Canine compatibility: Leashed dogs permitted
Fees and permits: Entrance fee
Schedule: Access is via the Scenic Drive, which is open daily Nov 1–Feb 28/29, 6 a.m.–5 p.m.;

Mar 1–Mar 31, 7 a.m.–7 p.m.; Apr 1–Sept 30, 6 a.m.–8 p.m.; Oct 1–Oct 31, 6 a.m.–7 p.m.
Maps: CalTopo.com MapBuilder Topo layer; USGS La Madre Spring, La Madre Mountain
Trail contacts: Bureau of Land Management, Red Rock/Sloan Canyon Field Office, 1000 Scenic Loop Dr., Las Vegas 89161; (702) 515-5350; https://www.blm.gov/visit/red-rock-canyon-national-conservation-area
Special considerations: During the summer hike early in the day and carry plenty of water.

Finding the trailhead: From the intersection of US 95 and I-15 in downtown Las Vegas, drive 5.1 miles west on US 95. Exit onto Summerlin Parkway and drive 3.8 miles west. Exit onto Town Center Drive and turn left. Continue 2.3 miles, and then turn right onto West Charleston Boulevard, NV 159. Continue 6.2 miles, and then turn right (north) on the Red Rock Canyon Scenic Drive. Drive 7.1 miles, then turn right onto the Willow Spring Picnic Area road. Continue 1.2 miles to the end of the paved road and park. GPS: N36 9.723'/W115 30.012'

The Hike

Walk up the Rocky Gap road, an unsigned jeep road that begins at the end of the pavement. Just after crossing the wash, turn right onto the La Madre Spring Trail, an old road. Follow the trail north along the west side of Red Rock Wash, the drainage at the foot of the White Rock Hills. Soon the trail veers left and follows the drainage below La Madre Spring. A small dam makes a catchment for the spring, and La Madre Spring is a few yards farther up the drainage. Bighorn sheep and many other forms of wildlife, including birds and deer, rely on the water from this spring.

For most animals, finding water in the desert is a life-or-death skill, one they must master. For most Americans, water is something that comes from a tap. Desert backpackers and explorers can't be quite so casual about water. In fact, desert backpack trips must be planned around known water sources, and alternative routes decided on if a water source is found to be dry. Some desert hiking routes are only possible when recent rains have filled water pockets or assured that seasonal streams and springs will be running. Of course, despite careful planning, it's always possible to find

Rock climbers ascending a crack in the canyon walls above the start of the La Madre Spring Trail. Red Rock Canyon is a world-class climbing area.

yourself in a situation where you need to find a water source in the desert. But before we go off on this water hunt, remember that if you are lost, injured, stranded, or otherwise unable to travel and you have enough water, stay in one place and wait for rescue. You'll drink much less water than you would searching for additional water.

If you must locate water, there are several possible water sources you can look for, including water pockets, natural tanks, springs, creeks, and man-made sources such as windmills. Water pockets and tanks are usually impossible to spot from a distance. The other sources can sometimes be spotted from a distance, if you know what to look for.

The best vantage point is high ground such as a ridge or a peak. A pair of binoculars is a big help. Scan the most likely areas, such as obvious drainages, and indicator plants such as cottonwood trees, willow, and tamarisk. Look toward the rising or setting sun for reflections from rain pockets or man-made stock tanks, or the reflection of a creek. Seasonal creeks may not have water-loving trees such as cottonwoods growing along them because the water only flows for a short time after a wet period. If you can look into a canyon, look for dark water streaks at pour-offs or dry falls. While the dark streak doesn't mean water is flowing now, it does mean water flows seasonally, and you may find water elsewhere along that same drainage.

As you walk along drainages looking for seasonal flows, natural tanks, and springs, keep an eye peeled for damp areas. Especially along the outside of bends or where bedrock forces groundwater close to the surface, you may be able to dig in a damp area and find water a few inches down. If this is the case, let the silt and mud settle out after digging the hole.

In the Basin and Range country, the mountains rise along fault lines, and these faults often cause water to rise to the surface in the form of springs where the steep slopes abruptly give way to outwash plains. Sometimes the opposite happens—permanent

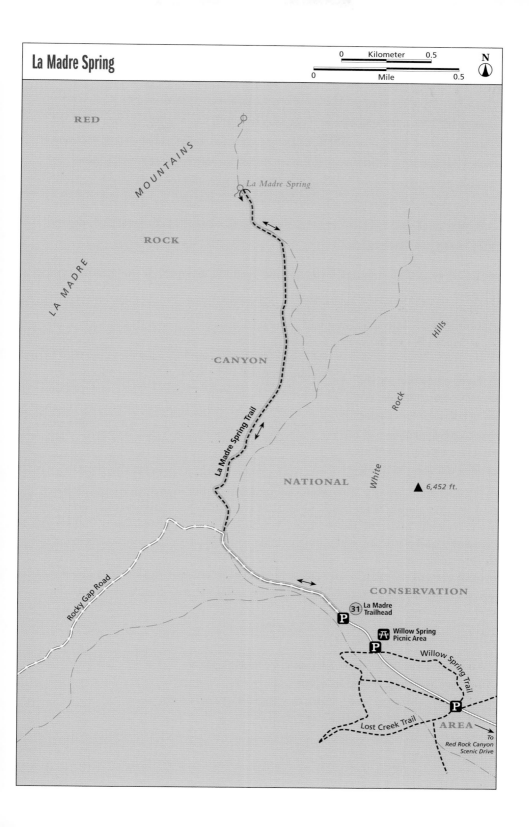

La Madre Spring

RED

MOUNTAINS

ROCK

LA MADRE

La Madre Spring

CANYON

Hills

White Rock

La Madre Spring Trail

NATIONAL

▲ 6,452 ft.

Rocky Gap Road

CONSERVATION

31 La Madre Trailhead

Willow Spring Picnic Area

Willow Spring Trail

Lost Creek Trail

AREA

To Red Rock Canyon Scenic Drive

N

0   Kilometer   0.5

0   Mile   0.5

VIEWING BIGHORN SHEEP

You'll have the best chance of seeing bighorn sheep, as well as other wildlife, if you remain quiet while hiking. Once you are at the water catchment, find a nearby vantage point and then sit or stand quietly. Concentrate on looking above you, as bighorn prefer higher terrain where they can see predators more easily. You'll often hear bighorn sheep moving before you actually catch sight of them, since they blend into their surroundings. If you do spot a band of sheep, a good pair of binoculars will help observe them more closely. Any attempt to approach will likely result in the bighorn demonstrating their sure-footed agility on rough terrain as they rapidly make their escape.

streams flow down a mountain canyon and abruptly disappear at the mouth of the canyon.

Don't overlook windmills. Ranchers drill wells and then install windmills to pump the water into a holding tank, which in turn feeds a watering trough. While some windmills have been abandoned, many others are still operating. Another artificial source is a water saver. These are generally built by wildlife agencies and consist of a rain-collection area made of metal, concrete, or plastic. The collected rainwater feeds into a holding tank and a watering trough. Though difficult to spot from a distance unless you are on a peak high above the surrounding terrain, they are worth knowing about in case you run across one.

▶ Purify all natural water sources before drinking or using the water for cooking. Use chemical purifier tablets, a hiker's water filter, or bring the water to a boil.

Many of the survival schemes that are often advanced for getting water in the deserts are not practical, such as getting water from a cactus or solar stills. Solar stills actually do work if you have the materials and the time. You'll need enough plastic sheets, collection containers, and plastic surgical tubing to build half a dozen or more solar stills in order to get enough water to survive hot weather. You're not likely to have the materials in your car when exploring, let alone in your pack when backpacking, and even if you do, you'll expend more body moisture making the stills than they can produce over several days.

Miles and Directions

0.0 From the end of the pavement, walk up the Rocky Gap Road.
0.5 Turn right onto La Madre Spring Trail.
1.9 Arrive at La Madre Spring, marked by a small dam. Return the way you came.
3.8 Arrive back at the end of the paved road.

32 North Peak

This hike leads to the rim of the Red Rock Escarpment above Icebox Canyon, a point that features excellent views of the numerous sandstone ridges and canyons of the Red Rock Canyon area.

Start: 29.2 miles west of Las Vegas
Distance: 2.4 miles out and back
Approximate hiking time: 2 hours
Difficulty: Moderate due to route finding
Trail surface: Dirt and rocks, cross-country, slickrock
Best season: All year
Water: None
Other trail users: None
Canine compatibility: Leashed dogs permitted
Fees and permits: Entrance fee
Schedule: Access is via the Scenic Drive, which is open daily Nov 1–Feb 28/29, 6 a.m.–5 p.m.;

Mar 1–Mar 31, 7 a.m.–7 p.m.; Apr 1–Sept 30, 6 a.m.–8 p.m.; Oct 1–Oct 31, 6 a.m.–7 p.m.
Maps: CalTopo.com MapBuilder Topo layer; USGS La Madre Spring, La Madre Mountain
Trail contacts: Bureau of Land Management, Red Rock/Sloan Canyon Field Office, 1000 Scenic Loop Dr., Las Vegas 89161; (702) 515-5350; https://www.blm.gov/visit/red-rock-canyon-national-conservation-area
Special considerations: During the summer hike early in the day and carry plenty of water.

Finding the trailhead: From the intersection of US 95 and I-15 in downtown Las Vegas, drive 5.1 miles west on US 95. Exit onto Summerlin Parkway and drive 3.8 miles west. Exit onto Town Center Drive and turn left. Continue 2.3 miles, and then turn right onto West Charleston Boulevard, NV 159. Continue 6.2 miles, and then turn right (north) on the Red Rock Canyon Scenic Drive. Drive 7.1 miles, then turn right onto the Willow Spring Picnic Area road. Continue 1.2 miles to the end of the paved road and the start of the unmaintained Rocky Gap Road. You'll need a high-clearance, four-wheel-drive vehicle to continue beyond this point. Drive 3.5 miles farther to Red Rock Summit. GPS: N36 7.822' / W115 32.005'

The Hike

The trail begins at Red Rock Summit and leaves the road to the east. It winds up around the head of a basin that drains to the west, and eventually reaches the crest of the escarpment. Here the trail to Bridge Mountain turns right; turn left and follow the ridge east–northeast to North Peak, a spectacular viewpoint at the head of Icebox Canyon. From this 7,208-foot summit the view encompasses the Spring Mountains to the north, the entire Red Rock Canyon area, Blue Diamond Mountain, the Las Vegas Valley, Lake Mead, the Mormon Mountains, and Mount Potosi. On clear days you can see the 8,000-foot Virgin Mountains 85 miles away in extreme northwestern Arizona.

The Spring Mountains, of which the Red Rock Escarpment is a part, is in the Great Basin and yet it isn't. "Great Basin" is defined several different ways, depending on whether you're considering hydrography, physical landforms, biology, or history,

Barrel cactus is common in the Red Rock Canyon area. Contrary to desert folklore, you cannot break open this cactus and find water inside. Instead, you'll find a bitter, pulpy flesh.

which is why many people are confused about the Great Basin's boundaries. The hydrographic Great Basin is the most precisely defined. It consists simply of that portion of the American West that drains internally. The streams and rivers of this Great Basin emerge from the mountains, run out into the intervening basins, and disappear into lakes, marshes, or, most commonly, salt flats, but they don't make it to the sea.

The Spring Mountains lie directly on the southwest boundary of the hydrographic Great Basin. The drainages on the northeast side of the range are tributaries of Las Vegas Wash and the Colorado River, which eventually flows into the Pacific Ocean, and so are not part of the Great Basin. The drainages on the southwest and west sides flow into the Pahrump Valley and just disappear into the desert floor, or end in salt flats (also known as playas). The next basin to the west is the headwaters of the Amargosa River, which sound impressive until you look at a map and realize that the Amargosa drains south, briefly west,

▶ In the dry desert air, normal visibility is in excess of 100 miles. Spring dust storms may drop the visibility to just a few miles as high winds pick up dust and spread it far and wide. Smog from nearby Las Vegas and even distant Los Angeles can also reduce the visibility, though not as drastically as dust storms. During the summer, smoke from forest fires can also drift over the region and reduce visibility, sometimes drastically if the fire is large or nearby.

THE KEYSTONE THRUST FAULT ZONE

This hike offers an excellent view of the Keystone Thrust fault zone. Tremendous forces associated with the movement of the earth's crustal plates have forced the dark gray limestones to ride up over the red and white sandstones that were formed later, and were originally positioned above the limestone. The limestone weathers into fairly large blocks that remain in place, trapping sand, silt, and plant debris, which develops into soil that supports a heavy cover of shrubs and small trees. The sandstone weathers differently, breaking down into sand grains that are easily washed and blown away, constantly exposing a new surface of solid rock that is bare of all plants except lichens and a few shrubs growing in cracks. The contrast between the brush-covered limestone and the bare sandstone beneath it clearly delineates the Keystone Thrust fault zone.

provide shelter for bird life. Amphibians such as frogs and toads breed in the ponds, and ravens, hawks, deer, bighorn sheep, and hundreds of other animals rely on the tinajas for water. People should never camp within 0.25 mile of such water sources, as the presence of humans will scare the wildlife away. Since there is no outlet from the tanks, pollutants from soap, human waste, or litter will remain in the basins indefinitely, poisoning the creatures that depend on these natural reservoirs.

From the large tank mentioned above, the trail becomes a mere route across the slickrock bench. The correct route is marked intermittently with small patches of orange paint in the shape of bighorn sheep tracks. If the correct route is not followed carefully, hikers will find themselves perched on the edge of a sheer drop with no way down. In many areas the route is broken by short vertical pitches that must be carefully negotiated. It is approximately 0.5 mile from the big tank to the bottom of the saddle that leads up to Bridge Mountain, with a drop of 350 feet.

To reach the bridge near the summit of Bridge Mountain, the route leads straight up a system of joints and ledges for a distance of 400 feet. The path is not as sheer as it appears during the approach, and there are plenty of holds for hands and feet. However, the climb is relatively exposed, and extreme care should be exercised during the climb. Hikers not comfortable with rock scrambling should turn back here. A misstep could plunge a hiker hundreds of feet into Pine Creek. Climbing within the joints offers more security, but climbing the faces alongside is slightly easier.

Once the bridge has been reached and explored, a further route leads up onto the bench above, from inside the alcove near the pine tree. Just 100 yards north of the bridge is a large, deep, nearly circular tinaja nearly 80 feet across and 60 feet deep. Over the bench to the east is a large alcove that shelters a hidden forest of ponderosa pines. Trees grow very slowly in this area because of the dry conditions. Wood is relatively scarce, slowly replaced, and absolutely should not be used to build fires. A fire in the hidden forest could cause damage that would not heal in a thousand

Bridge Mountain

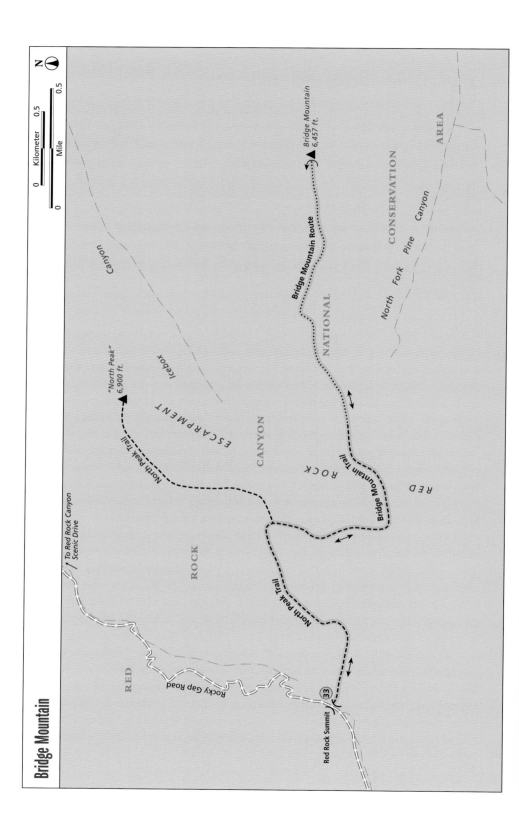

ROCK SCRAMBLING

Rock scrambling is a skill that can greatly extend your hiking range, allowing you to reach summits and places without a trail. As soon as rock becomes steep enough to require the use of your hands, test all doubtful holds before trusting them with your full weight. Always maintain three points of contact—that is, keep all but one hand or foot on good holds and move only one hand or foot at a time. That way, if a hold breaks or you lose your grip, you'll still have two points of contact with the rock. As you climb, keep your weight over your feet and do not lean forward. Leaning forward pushes your feet outward on their holds and actually decreases your security. By using your leg muscles to climb and your hands and arms for balance, you'll save a lot of energy.

years. Note that all wood gathering and ground fires are prohibited in the Red Rock backcountry.

Return to Red Rock Summit by retracing your route. Do not attempt to take shortcuts or alternate routes.

Note: This hike description was provided by the Bureau of Land Management.

Miles and Directions

0.0 Leave Red Rock Summit and follow the informal trail to the east.

0.3 The trail swings north through a small basin and then climbs onto a ridge to the north.

0.4 Follow the trail up the ridge to the northeast.

1.1 Reach the crest of the escarpment. Turn right and follow the informal trail along the ridge to the south.

2.3 Arrive at the saddle below Bridge Mountain. Hikers not comfortable with rock scrambling should turn back here.

3.0 Arrive at Bridge Mountain. Return the way you came.

6.0 Arrive back at Red Rock Summit.

GREEN TIP:
Go out of your way to avoid birds and animals that are mating or taking care of their young.

34 White Rock–Willow Spring Trail

This hike takes you along the base of the White Rock Hills to a rare desert spring. Bighorn sheep frequent the slopes of the White Rock Hills above the spring.

Start: 25.0 miles west of Las Vegas
Distance: 3.4 miles out and back
Approximate hiking time: 2 hours
Difficulty: Easy
Trail surface: Dirt and rocks, old road
Best season: All year
Water: None
Other trail users: None
Canine compatibility: Leashed dogs permitted
Fees and permits: Entrance fee
Schedule: Access is via the Scenic Drive, which is open daily Nov 1–Feb 28/29, 6 a.m.–5 p.m.; Mar 1–Mar 31, 7 a.m.–7 p.m.; Apr 1–Sept 30, 6 a.m.–8 p.m.; Oct 1–Oct 31, 6 a.m.–7 p.m.

Maps: CalTopo.com MapBuilder Topo layer; USGS La Madre Mountain
Trail contacts: Bureau of Land Management, Red Rock/Sloan Canyon Field Office, 1000 Scenic Loop Dr., Las Vegas 89161; (702) 515-5350; https://www.blm.gov/visit/red-rock-canyon-national-conservation-area
Special considerations: During the summer hike early in the day and carry plenty of water.

Finding the trailhead: From the intersection of US 95 and I-15 in downtown Las Vegas, drive 5.1 miles west on US 95. Exit onto Summerlin Parkway and drive 3.8 miles west. Exit onto Town Center Drive and turn left. Continue 2.3 miles, and then turn right onto West Charleston Boulevard, NV 159. Continue 6.2 miles, and then turn right (north) on the Red Rock Canyon Scenic Drive. Drive 7.1 miles, then turn right onto the Willow Spring Picnic Area Road. Continue 0.5 mile to the Lost Creek Trailhead, on the left. GPS: N36 9.445' / W115 29.593'

The Hike

From the Lost Creek Trailhead, cross the road to the White Rock–Willow Spring Trail. Follow the trail to the northeast along the base of the White Rock Hills. The trail turns north to remain near the base of the White Rock Hills. Finally, the trail turns to the northeast again and reaches the junction with the White Rock Spring Trail. Turn left, and walk the White Rock Spring Trail a short distance to White Rock Spring.

At the spring a rectangular cement basin catches the water from the spring and provides a much-needed water source for desert bighorn sheep and other animals. The improvements to the spring were originally made by the Civilian Conservation Corps during the 1930s. The rocky hillsides of the White Rock Hills are a good place to observe bighorn sheep in season.

Animals have a number of strategies for coping with the desert's heat and dryness. Many are nocturnal, at least during the summer, but others are active day and night. One such desert dweller is the tiny antelope ground squirrel, commonly seen aboveground and active on hot summer days. Unlike most squirrels, it is omnivorous, eating water-rich animal parts as well as plants. Instead of panting, the squirrel drools,

148

WATER-SAVERS

Desert bighorn sheep require large areas of rugged mountains in order to survive. They also depend on rare desert water sources such as White Rock Spring. In areas that are prime sheep habitat, wildlife managers not only develop springs such as this one, they also create additional water sources by installing water-savers. A water-saver consists of a rain collector constructed of sheet metal, concrete, or plastic that drains into a holding tank, which in turn feeds a watering trough. The water-saver is fenced to keep domestic stock from competing with wildlife. Why do we need to build water sources for wild animals that existed for thousands of years without our help? Because we have eliminated much of their habitat with our activities. Endangered animals such as desert bighorn sheep now depend on our efforts to conserve them.

drools, which wets some of its chest fur and provides evaporative cooling. It also takes advantage of cooler microclimates such as the shade of bushes or rocks, and climbs up bushes or trees to escape the extreme ground heat. Most small animals cannot store much excess body heat, but the antelope ground squirrel can, at least for short periods. It retreats to its underground burrow several times an hour to spread out on the cool dirt.

Jackrabbits stay aboveground during the daytime heat, staying cool by resting in the shade and flattening their large ears along their backs. They have unusually large and light-colored ears with many blood vessels, which reflect light and heat and also act as radiators to dissipate heat. Jackrabbits forage at night. In some cases they can survive without drinking liquid water by getting moisture from green plants.

The kangaroo rat, named for its strong hind legs and incredible jumping ability, is remarkable in another way. It can live its entire life without drinking water at all, obtaining all the water it needs by metabolizing dry plant food. To do this, it adopts extreme moisture conservation. It is active at night, and

The La Madre Mountains loom above the White Rock Hills.

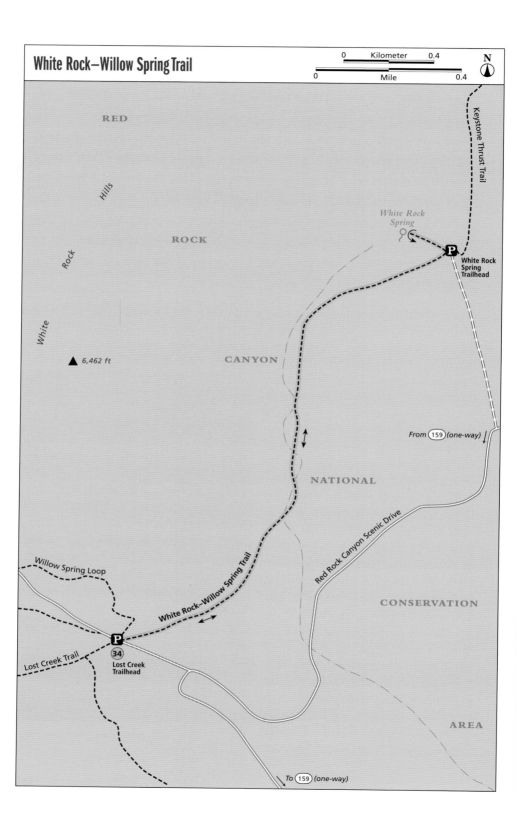

White Rock–Willow Spring Trail

| 0 | Kilometer | 0.4 |
| 0 | Mile | 0.4 |

N

RED

Hills

Rock

White

ROCK

▲ 6,462 ft

CANYON

White Rock
Spring

Keystone Thrust Trail

P White Rock
Spring
Trailhead

From 159 (one-way)

NATIONAL

Red Rock Canyon Scenic Drive

Willow Spring Loop

White Rock–Willow Spring Trail

CONSERVATION

Lost Creek Trail

P
34
Lost Creek
Trailhead

AREA

To 159 (one-way)

during the day it plugs the entrance to its burrow, which raises the humidity within the burrow several times higher than the outside humidity. The kangaroo rat's nasal passages are cooler than its body temperature. When it inhales, evaporation cools the nasal tissues. In the lungs the air is saturated with moisture at the higher body temperature. During exhalation, the air passes through the cooler nasal passages and loses some of its moisture. In addition the kangaroo

White Rock Spring is a rare permanent water source at the foot of the White Rock Hills. Desert bighorn sheep and many other animals depend on such widely separated desert water sources.

rat's feces are dry and firm with little wasted moisture, and its urine is four to five times more concentrated than a human's.

Another desert heat-avoiding strategy is estivation, which is similar to winter hibernation in that it lets the animal avoid severe environmental conditions. In both hibernation and estivation, the animal becomes torpid and its body temperature drops to a few degrees above the ambient temperature in its burrow. Oxygen intake drops and metabolism slows, which conserves energy. There are some small desert mammals that estivate on a daily cycle.

Humans, having evolved in a wetter climate, are poorly adapted to the desert. On the other hand we are capable of changing our habits and inventing technology to deal with the heat and lack of water. Unfortunately, using inventions such as air-conditioning and massive water projects to transform the desert environment to something more to our liking, at least within our cities, disconnects us from the reality of the desert. The hiker who rests in the shade for a few hours during the hottest part of the day is wisely adapting a strategy used by desert nomads for thousands of years, and still practiced in hot climates in the form of the siesta.

Miles and Directions

0.0   From the Lost Creek Trailhead, cross the road and start on the White Rock–Willow Springs Trail.

1.6   At the White Rock Spring Trail Junction, turn left on the White Rock Spring Trail.

1.7   Arrive at White Rock Spring. Return the way you came.

3.4   Arrive back at the Lost Creek Trailhead.

GREEN TIP:
Never feed wild animals under any circumstances. You will damage their health and expose yourself (and them) to danger.

35 Lost Creek Loop-Children's Discovery Trail

This loop hike to a box canyon features a seasonal waterfall and a panel of prehistoric pictographs. The waterfall is best in the spring after a snowy winter provides plenty of snowmelt.

Start: 25.0 miles west of Las Vegas
Distance: 1.2-mile loop
Approximate hiking time: 1 hour
Difficulty: Easy
Trail surface: Dirt and rocks
Best season: All year
Water: None
Other trail users: None
Canine compatibility: Leashed dogs permitted
Fees and permits: Entrance fee
Schedule: Access is via the Scenic Drive, which is open daily Nov 1–Feb 28/29, 6 a.m.–5 p.m.; Mar 1–Mar 31, 7 a.m.–7 p.m.; Apr 1–Sept 30, 6 a.m.–8 p.m.; Oct 1–Oct 31, 6 a.m.–7 p.m.
Maps: CalTopo.com MapBuilder Topo layer; USGS La Madre Mountain
Trail contacts: Bureau of Land Management, Red Rock/Sloan Canyon Field Office, 1000 Scenic Loop Dr., Las Vegas 89161; (702) 515-5350; https://www.blm.gov/visit/red-rock-canyon-national-conservation-area
Special considerations: During the summer hike early in the day and carry plenty of water.

Finding the trailhead: From the intersection of US 95 and I-15 in downtown Las Vegas, drive 5.1 miles west on US 95. Exit onto Summerlin Parkway and drive 3.8 miles west. Exit onto Town Center Drive and turn left. Continue 2.3 miles, and then turn right onto West Charleston Boulevard, NV 159. Continue 6.2 miles, and then turn right (north) on the Red Rock Canyon Scenic Drive. Drive 7.1 miles, then turn right onto the Willow Spring Picnic Area road. Continue 0.5 mile to the Lost Creek Trailhead, on the left. GPS: N36 9.445'/W115 29.593'

The Hike

From the trailhead, start on the Lost Creek Trail by crossing the wash to the west. After the wash the trail climbs into an unnamed canyon and soon reaches a seasonal waterfall at the head of a box canyon. The loop continues along the north side of the canyon, where the trail passes a panel of pictographs. The Lost Creek Trail descends north to the wash, and then turns east to return to the Lost Creek Trailhead.

All children and many adults love a treasure hunt. A high-tech form of treasure hunting, geocaching, has caught on in a big way, using Global Positioning System (GPS) receivers to hunt for hidden caches left by other people. Although the sport of geocaching predates the availability of GPS to civilians, GPS has made geocaching a lot more fun and appealing to a large number of people. Geocaches can be placed by anyone and located anywhere, from city to countryside, where their presence is legal. (**FYI:** National parks prohibit the placement of geocaches, as do National Wilderness Areas.)

36 Base of the Escarpment

This trail winds along the base of the Red Rock Escarpment from Lost Creek to Oak Creek Canyon using a series of interconnecting trails. It offers excellent views of the rock faces of the escarpment as well as distant views of La Madre Mountain, the White Rock Hills, Turtlehead Peak, and the Calico Hills.

Start: 25.0 miles west of Las Vegas
Distance: 9.6 miles out and back
Approximate hiking time: 5 hours
Difficulty: Moderate due to length
Trail surface: Dirt and rocks
Best season: All year
Water: None
Other trail users: None
Canine compatibility: Leashed dogs permitted
Fees and permits: Entrance fee
Schedule: Access is via the Scenic Drive, which is open daily Nov 1–Feb 28/29, 6 a.m.–5 p.m.;

Mar 1–Mar 31, 7 a.m.–7 p.m.; Apr 1–Sept 30, 6 a.m.–8 p.m.; Oct 1–Oct 31, 6 a.m.–7 p.m.
Maps: CalTopo.com MapBuilder Topo layer; USGS Blue Diamond, La Madre Mountain
Trail contacts: Bureau of Land Management, Red Rock/Sloan Canyon Field Office, 1000 Scenic Loop Dr., Las Vegas 89161; (702) 515-5350; https://www.blm.gov/visit/red-rock-canyon-national-conservation-area
Special considerations: During the summer hike early in the day and carry plenty of water.

Finding the trailhead: From the Oak Creek Trailhead, turn left on NV 159 and drive 2.6 miles. Turn left on the Red Rock Canyon Scenic Drive. Drive 7.1 miles, then turn right onto the Willow Spring Picnic Area road. Continue 0.5 mile to the Lost Creek Trailhead, on the left. GPS: N36 9.445'/W115 29.593'

The Hike

Start on the left-hand branch of the Lost Creek Trail, and then turn left on the SMYC Trail, which crosses Red Rock Wash and heads south toward the base of the Red Rock Escarpment. Once on the slopes below the escarpment, the SMYC Trail turns southeast and wanders along the base of the escarpment to end at the Icebox Canyon Trail.

Cross the Icebox Canyon Trail and start on the Dales Trail, which continues to skirt the base of the escarpment in a southeasterly direction. Old roads confuse this section; when in doubt, stay close to the base of the escarpment. The Dales Trail turns more to the south as it approaches the mouth of Pine Creek Canyon. The trail ends at the Pine Creek Trail; turn right and follow the Pine Creek Trail west toward the mouth of Pine Creek Canyon.

At the ruins of the old homestead, the Pine Creek Trail splits to form a loop. Turn left on the Pine Creek Trail and cross Pine Creek, where you'll meet the Arnight Trail. Turn left on the Arnight Trail to continue the hike along the base of the escarpment.

The Arnight Trail crosses a drainage below an unnamed canyon cutting west into the escarpment, and turns southeast away from the escarpment. As the terrain levels out into a sage flat, the Arnight Trail reaches the Oak Creek Trailhead. Retrace your steps to the Lost Creek Trailhead.

Although Red Rock Canyon is not in the hydrographic Great Basin, the area where rivers have no outlet to the sea and all drainage ends in valleys and sinks, they are part of another Great Basin—the physiographic one, which is more commonly known as the Basin and Range geological province. Looking at the area from the point of view of a geologist or, more precisely, a physiographer, what links the area together is not the drainage pattern but the similarities of the mountains and valleys.

The SMYC Trail connects the Lost Creek Trailhead to the Icebox Canyon Trailhead, and winds along the base of the escarpment.

The Basin and Range province is a large area of the intermountain West where the topography consists of parallel, generally north–south-trending mountain ranges and broad intervening valleys. Southern and western Arizona, part of southeastern California, nearly all of Nevada, part of southeastern Oregon, southern Idaho, and western Utah are Basin and Range. Although the borders are not as clearly defined as that of the hydrographic Great Basin, they are generally accepted as the Sierra Nevada and the Cascade Mountains on the west, the Columbia Plateau to the north, and the Rocky Mountains to the east. It is on the southern boundary that the difficulties begin. Most physiographers include southeastern California in the Basin and Range, but not everyone agrees that western and southern Arizona should be included. One reason for this is that the generally north–south orientation of the mountains and valleys breaks down in Arizona, where some ranges run east–west.

▶ To avoid an out-and-back hike or a car shuttle between two trailheads, if your group is large enough (four or more is good), split your group in half and use two vehicles. One group drives to one trailhead and the other group to the other trailhead. Meet along the trail and swap keys.

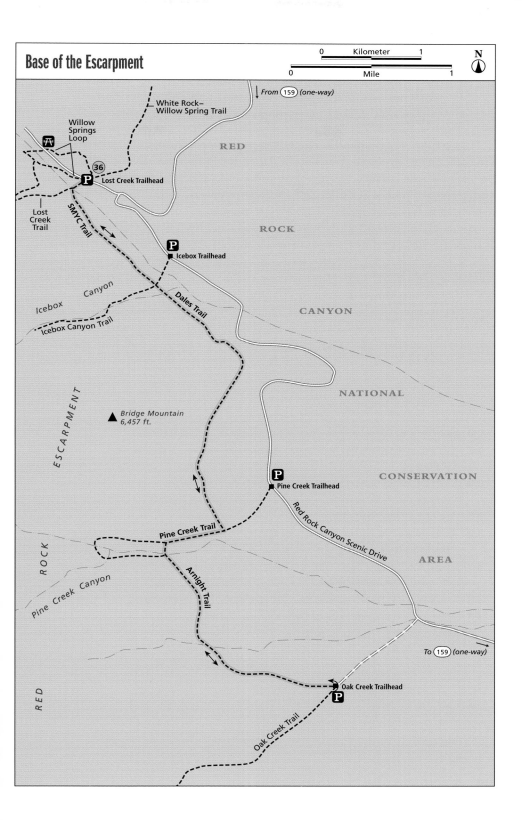

Base of the Escarpment

0   Kilometer   1

0   Mile   1

N

White Rock–
Willow Spring Trail

From 159 *(one-way)*

RED

Willow
Springs
Loop

36

Lost Creek Trailhead

ROCK

Lost
Creek
Trail

SMYC Trail

Icebox Trailhead

Canyon

Dales Trail

Icebox

Icebox Canyon Trail

CANYON

ESCARPMENT

▲ *Bridge Mountain*
6,457 ft.

NATIONAL

Pine Creek Trailhead

CONSERVATION

Red Rock Canyon Scenic Drive

Pine Creek Trail

ROCK

AREA

Pine Creek Canyon

Arnight Trail

To 159 *(one-way)*

RED

Oak Creek Trailhead

Oak Creek Trail

The parallel, long mountain ranges and valleys were formed by faulting during the collision of the Pacific and North American Plates. During this collision the Basin and Range country was stretched from east to west, and the crust broke along north–south fault lines. Some blocks sank to form valleys, while others rose and tilted to form fault-block mountains.

Although the general impression is that Basin and Range mountains are low and lack much relief, in reality many of them are above 10,000 feet, including the Spring Mountains, of which Red Rock Canyon is a part. The Spring Mountains rise more than 10,600 feet above Lake Mead, and the rise from the bottom of Death Valley to the top of White Mountain Peak in California is over 14,500 feet. Wheeler Peak in the Snake Range, at 13,068 feet the second-highest point in Nevada (Boundary Peak at the north end of the White Mountains is the highest, at 13,130 feet), rises more than 8,000 feet above the valley to the northeast. Of course, as you hike along the base of the Red Rock Escarpment and its 3,000-foot rise, the relief is dramatic and inescapable.

Miles and Directions

0.0 From the Lost Creek Trailhead, start on the left fork of the Lost Creek Trail.

0.1 Turn left on the SMYC Trail and follow it south toward the base of the Red Rock Escarpment.

0.9 Cross the Icebox Canyon Trail and start on the Dales Trail, which crosses the Icebox Canyon drainage and continues along the base of the Red Rock Escarpment.

2.8 Turn right on the Pine Creek Trail.

3.2 At the ruins of the old homestead, turn right on the left fork of the Pine Creek Trail and cross Pine Creek.

3.3 On the south side of Pine Creek, turn left on the Arnight Trail and follow it along the base of the Red Rock Escarpment.

3.9 The Arnight Trail turns southeast away from the base of the escarpment.

4.8 Arrive at the Oak Creek Trailhead. Return the way you came.

9.6 Arrive back at the Lost Creek Trailhead.

37 Icebox Canyon

Featuring a seasonal waterfall and box canyon, this short hike nevertheless takes you deep into the towering cliffs of the Red Rock Escarpment.

Start: 25.4 miles west of Las Vegas
Distance: 2.2 miles out and back
Approximate hiking time: 2 hours
Difficulty: Easy
Trail surface: Dirt and rocks, boulder-hopping
Best season: All year
Water: None
Other trail users: None
Canine compatibility: Leashed dogs permitted
Fees and permits: Entrance fee
Schedule: Access is via the Scenic Drive, which is open daily Nov 1–Feb 28/29, 6 a.m.–5 p.m.;

Mar 1–Mar 31, 7 a.m.–7 p.m.; Apr 1–Sept 30, 6 a.m.–8 p.m.; Oct 1–Oct 31, 6 a.m.–7 p.m.
Maps: CalTopo.com MapBuilder Topo layer; USGS La Madre Mountain
Trail contacts: Bureau of Land Management, Red Rock/Sloan Canyon Field Office, 1000 Scenic Loop Dr., Las Vegas 89161; (702) 515-5350; https://www.blm.gov/visit/red-rock-canyon-national-conservation-area
Special considerations: During the summer hike early in the day and carry plenty of water.

Finding the trailhead: From the intersection of US 95 and I-15 in downtown Las Vegas, drive 5.1 miles west on US 95. Exit onto Summerlin Parkway and drive 3.8 miles west. Exit onto Town Center Drive and turn left. Continue 2.3 miles, and then turn right onto West Charleston Boulevard, NV 159. Continue 6.2 miles, and then turn right (north) on the Red Rock Canyon Scenic Drive. Drive 8.0 miles to the Icebox Canyon Trailhead, on the right. GPS: N36 9.017'/W115 29.049'

The Hike

From the trailhead, the Icebox Canyon Trail descends to cross Red Rock Wash and follows the Icebox Canyon drainage upstream, generally staying on the north side of the bed. When the canyon narrows, the trail drops into the wash. Boulder-hop up the wash to a seasonal waterfall and box canyon. Icebox Canyon derives its name from the cooler temperatures in this narrow canyon.

The main reason Icebox Canyon is so much cooler and lusher than the open desert below is due to the effect of microclimates. A microclimate is a small area, such as a canyon, valley, or slope aspect, that has a different climate than the surrounding area. Microclimates are often present in canyons such as Icebox Canyon because of cold air flowing down the canyon.

▶ Seasonal waterfalls are found all over Nevada in the numerous canyons that cut into the flanks of the mountains. At higher elevations the falls run during the snowmelt of late spring and early summer, and sometimes briefly after heavy thunderstorms. At lower elevations such as these, the falls tend to be at their best during runoff from wet, winter storms, which occur from December through March.

▶ During calm periods and especially at night, heavier, denser cold air flows down mountain canyons. These cooler temperatures create microclimates, small areas where the year-round climate differs enough from the surrounding area to support a plant and animal community normally found at higher elevations. An example is the presence of ponderosa pines along the canyon, trees that are heat- and drought-resistant but do require a certain amount of water to survive. The shady depths of Icebox Canyon retard evaporation and provide a moister climate than the surrounding open desert.

As the sun sets, the ground begins to lose its daytime heat by radiating heat to the sky in the form of infrared radiation. This causes the air near the surface to cool, and since cool air is heavier than warm air, the cool air begins to flow downhill. At Red Rock Canyon cool air flows down the mountain slopes and collects in the canyons and valleys below. Cool air collecting in valleys often forms an inversion, which is a layer of cool air trapped under a layer of warmer air. The process is most active on clear, calm nights. Wind interrupts the processing by mixing the lower atmosphere, and clouds slow or stop radiation to the sky.

Because cool air holds less moisture than warm air, the cool air that collects in canyons and valleys tends to have higher relative humidity, which in turn helps the soil retain moisture. Cool humid air and moist soil favors plants that cannot grow on warmer, drier open slopes. Even small canyons can be 10 or 20 degrees Fahrenheit cooler than the slopes just above the canyon bottom.

Microclimates are also present on opposite slopes of a canyon, a ridge, or a peak, especially if those slopes face north and south. Because the sun is in the southern sky (in the Northern Hemisphere), it shines more directly on south-facing slopes and makes these slopes hotter and drier than level areas. The opposite is true on north-facing slopes, where the lower sun angle results in less heating, so these slopes are both cooler and moister than level areas.

Rain shadow effects also contribute to microclimates. Usually, windward slopes are wetter than lee slopes, because air rises and

Icebox Creek cascades over boulders during the winter and spring months, but is usually dry during the summer.

Icebox Canyon

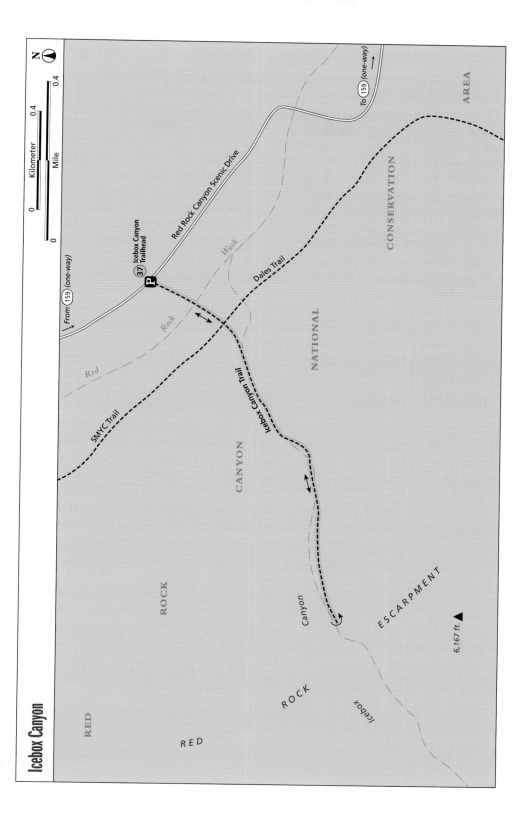

RED ROCK

RED

RED ROCK CANYON NATIONAL CONSERVATION AREA

ROCK CANYON

ESCARPMENT

6,167 ft. ▲

Icebox Canyon

Icebox

SMYC Trail

Icebox Canyon Trail

Dales Trail

Red Rock Wash

Rock

Red

Red Rock Canyon Scenic Drive

From 159 (one-way)

To 159 (one-way)

37 Icebox Canyon Trailhead

P

N

0   0.4   Kilometer

0   0.4   Mile

cools as it ascends a slope, and that increases the humidity of the air and also increases precipitation.

Smaller-scale microclimates form under rock overhangs, under trees, and even under bushes. Backpackers and hikers can take advantage of microclimates to have a more comfortable camp or even a nicer lunch stop. Because the ground radiates primarily to the open sky, camping under a dense tree or partially or completely under a rock overhang blocks much of the radiation. It can be as much as 20 degrees warmer under a tree than next to it in the open.

Along canyon bottoms, in many cases you can escape the damp chill air by climbing just 20 to 50 feet above the canyon bottom to camp on a ledge or other handy place. You'll also get the sun earlier than you would in the canyon bottom. The classic day hiker's lunch stop in the shade of a tree on a hot day can be made even cooler by selecting a spot in the shade of a large cliff.

Miles and Directions

0.0   Leave the Icebox Canyon Trailhead on the Icebox Canyon Trail.

0.2   Cross the SMYC and Dales Trails; continue straight ahead on the Icebox Canyon Trail.

1.1   Arrive at the seasonal waterfall. Return the way you came.

2.2   Arrive back at the Icebox Canyon Trailhead.

38 Pine Creek Canyon

Extensive stands of ponderosa pine give this canyon its name. The trail also leads past a pioneer homestead site and then loops past the confluence of the north and south forks of Pine Creek.

Start: 28.0 miles west of Last Vegas
Distance: 2.5-mile loop with a cherry stem
Approximate hiking time: 2 hours
Difficulty: Easy
Trail surface: Dirt and rocks
Best season: All year
Water: Pine Creek
Other trail users: None
Canine compatibility: Leashed dogs permitted
Fees and permits: Entrance fee
Schedule: Access is via the Scenic Drive, which is open daily Nov 1–Feb 28/29, 6 a.m.–5 p.m.;

Mar 1–Mar 31, 7 a.m.–7 p.m.; Apr 1–Sept 30, 6 a.m.–8 p.m.; Oct 1–Oct 31, 6 a.m.–7 p.m.
Maps: CalTopo.com MapBuilder Topo layer; USGS Blue Diamond, La Madre Mountain
Trail contacts: Bureau of Land Management, Red Rock/Sloan Canyon Field Office, 1000 Scenic Loop Dr., Las Vegas 89161; (702) 515-5350; https://www.blm.gov/visit/red-rock-canyon-national-conservation-area
Special considerations: During the summer hike early in the day and carry plenty of water.

Finding the trailhead: From the intersection of US 95 and I-15 in downtown Las Vegas, drive 5.1 miles west on US 95. Exit onto Summerlin Parkway and drive 3.8 miles west. Exit onto Town Center Drive and turn left. Continue 2.3 miles, and then turn right onto West Charleston Boulevard, NV 159. Continue 6.2 miles, and then turn right (north) on the Red Rock Canyon Scenic Drive. Drive 10.6 miles to the Pine Creek Trailhead, on the right. GPS: N36 7.717'/W115 28.402'

The Hike

From the Pine Creek Trailhead, follow the trail downhill below the bluff. The trail then follows the north side of Pine Creek west toward the mouth of Pine Creek Canyon. Continue straight on the Pine Creek Trail when you pass the junction with the Dales Trail. Just before you enter the mouth of the canyon, you'll come to the old Horace Wilson homestead site; nothing remains except the foundation. Pioneer families picked sites like this to homestead because of the water source and the cooler climate, which gave them a better chance of successfully growing crops and raising domesticated animals.

The loop portion of the trail starts at the homestead site; stay right to hike the loop counterclockwise. The Pine Creek Trail stays on the north side of Pine Creek as it heads toward the confluence of the north and south forks of Pine Creek. Mature yellow-barked ponderosa pines grow in the mouth of the canyon, well below their normal elevation range in this area.

At the confluence of the two forks of Pine Creek, turn left and cross the creek to follow the return loop. The trail stays on the south side of Pine Creek until it reaches

The ruins of an old homestead mark the beginning of the loop trail portion of the hike into Pine Creek Canyon.

the Arnight Trail; turn left and follow the Pine Creek Trail north across Pine Creek to the homestead site. Then turn right to return to the Pine Creek Trailhead.

Between 1862 and 1934, 1.6 million homesteads were granted covering 270 million acres, which is 10 percent of all the land in the United States. Many of the ranches still operating in Nevada started as homesteads.

The purpose of the original Homestead Act of 1862 was to encourage the settlement of the lands west of the original thirteen colonies. By filing an application, making specified improvements to the land, living on the land for five years, and filing for deed of title, a homesteader could acquire 160 acres (0.25 square mile) of federal land.

As the rich river bottom land in the east was all settled, and homesteaders started filing claims in the western Great Plains and in the West, a major problem became apparent with the original Homestead Act. One hundred sixty acres simply wasn't enough land to support a family on land where rainfall was insufficient to grow crops. As a result, two major expansions of the Homestead Act were passed by Congress. The Enlarged Homestead Act in 1909 increased the number of acres that could be claimed to 320, in order to facilitate dry land farming. The Stock-Raising Homestead Act of 1916 allowed 640 acres, or 1 square mile, to allow for raising stock.

SINGING PINES

Ponderosa pines are easily identified by both their bark and their needles. The bark is rough and furrowed, and it's made up of numerous small plates that resemble the pieces of a puzzle. Young trees have dark gray bark, while on older, larger trees the bark turns orangeish in color. Ponderosa pine needles are 5 to 7 inches long and grow in bunches of three. In a wind the long needles give a soft singing sound to the breeze in a ponderosa pine stand, in contrast to the harsher, more alpine sound given off by short-needled fir and spruce trees.

MICROCLIMATE

The microclimate supporting the tall pines is caused by the high canyon walls, which increase the amount of shade, the moisture from the Pine Creek drainage, and the cool air flowing down the canyon at night. After sunset on calm clear nights, the ground in the high mountains rapidly cools by radiating its heat to the open sky. This in turn cools the air in contact with the earth. The cool air is heavier than warmer air and starts to flow downward, collecting in the drainages and moving toward the valleys via the canyons. This is why there is often a down-canyon breeze or even a wind in desert canyons and mountain valleys after sunset. The cool air fills the valley bottoms, forming a nighttime inversion trapping the cool, moist air under the warmer air aloft. If you hike into Pine Creek Canyon around sunrise on a calm morning, you can feel a 10- or even 20-degree temperature drop as you near the drainage.

Still, more than half of all homestead claims failed because poor sites were chosen or because 640 acres was far too small a plot for a family to make a living in most areas of the West. Most successful western cattle ranches ended up running their cattle on public land and paying a grazing fee to the government.

Of course, there were many abuses and illegal uses of the homestead laws. Since ranching in the West required the control of so much land, a common tactic was for an individual fronting for a large ranching operation to file a homestead claim on a major spring or other valuable water source so that the ranch could in effect control all the surrounding land. Fraudulent homestead claims were also used to gain private ownership of land with timber or oil

Sandstone cliffs in Pine Creek Canyon

Pine Creek Canyon

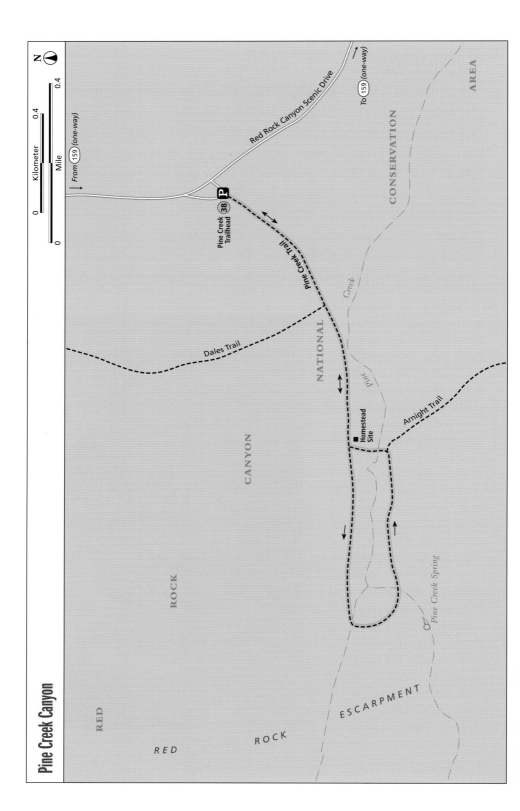

N

Kilometer
0   0.4

Mile
0   0.4

From 159 (one-way)

Red Rock Canyon Scenic Drive

To 159 (one-way)

Pine Creek Trailhead 38

P

Pine Creek Trail

Dales Trail

Creek

Pine

Homestead Site

Arnight Trail

Pine Creek Spring

RED ROCK CANYON NATIONAL CONSERVATION AREA

RED ROCK ESCARPMENT

resources. For example, much of the rain forest timberlands west of Portland, Oregon, were acquired by misuse of the homestead laws. In practice, there was little oversight of homestead claims because of the vastness of the lands involved. Land offices really had no choice but to rely on statements made by witnesses that the land had been improved and lived on for the required period.

Although not illegal, large estates were built up when the children of homesteaders came of age and filed claims on the land adjoining their parents' original claim.

Miles and Directions

0.0 Leave the Pine Creek Trailhead on the Pine Creek Trail, which descends the bluff below the trailhead.

0.3 Dales Trail comes in from the right (north); continue straight ahead on the Pine Creek Trail.

0.7 Pass the Horace Wilson homestead site, on the left and the return portion of the loop trail. Continue straight ahead.

1.2 The Pine Creek Trail crosses Pine Creek near the confluence of the north and south forks of Pine Creek.

1.7 At the Arnight Trail junction, stay left on the Pine Creek Trail and cross Pine Creek.

1.8 At Horace Wilson homestead site, turn right to return to the main trail and the trailhead.

2.5 Arrive back at the Pine Creek Trailhead.

39 Oak Creek Canyon

This day hike in the Red Rock Canyon National Conservation Area features stands of live shrub oak.

Start: 30.0 miles west of Las Vegas
Distance: 2.8 miles out and back
Approximate hiking time: 2 hours
Difficulty: Easy
Trail surface: Old road, dirt and rocks
Best season: All year
Water: None
Other trail users: None
Canine compatibility: Leashed dogs permitted
Fees and permits: Entrance fee
Schedule: Access is via the Scenic Drive, which is open daily Nov 1–Feb 28/29, 6 a.m.–5 p.m.; Mar 1–Mar 31, 7 a.m.–7 p.m.; Apr 1–Sept 30, 6 a.m.–8 p.m.; Oct 1–Oct 31, 6 a.m.–7 p.m.
Maps: CalTopo.com MapBuilder Topo layer; USGS Blue Diamond
Trail contacts: Bureau of Land Management, Red Rock/Sloan Canyon Field Office, 1000 Scenic Loop Dr., Las Vegas 89161; (702) 515-5350; https://www.blm.gov/visit/red-rock-canyon-national-conservation-area
Special considerations: During the summer hike early in the day and carry plenty of water.

Finding the trailhead: From the intersection of US 95 and I-15 in downtown Las Vegas, drive 5.1 miles west on US 95. Exit onto Summerlin Parkway and drive 3.8 miles west. Exit onto Town Center Drive and turn left. Continue 2.3 miles, and then turn right onto West Charleston Boulevard, NV 159. Continue 6.2 miles, and then turn right (north) on the Red Rock Canyon Scenic Drive. Drive 11.9 miles, and then turn right on the Oak Creek Trailhead road. Drive 0.7 mile to the Oak Creek Trailhead at the end of the road. GPS: N36 6.663' / W115 27.980'

The Hike

From the Oak Creek Trailhead, the Oak Creek Trail heads southwest toward Oak Creek. As the trail nears Oak Creek, it meets an old road coming in from the east, which is the Old Oak Creek Trail. Turn right to follow the Oak Creek Trail directly toward the mouth of Oak Creek. The trail ends just after passing Oak Creek Spring; return the way you came.

A major alien invasion is taking place in Nevada and the West. Rather than a dramatic War of the Worlds, it's mostly a silent invasion of exotic, non–native plants. Alien plants are plants that did not naturally occur in the area, and have been brought over from other continents. Some alien plants were brought over on purpose as ornamentals, while others were accidental, entering with shipments of grain or other items.

The problem with many alien plants is that they outcompete and replace native species, use vast amounts of water, increase fire hazards, invade crops, increase erosion, and often have little value to native wildlife.

Cheatgrass, an exotic grass from the Mediterranean, grows in sagebrush–covered valleys such as the valley below the Red Rock Escarpment. In the last twenty years,

Snow dusts the top of Rainbow Mountain above the mouth of Oak Creek Canyon.

cheatgrass has spread through much of the sagebrush country in Nevada, increasing the intensity and coverage of wildfires. Sagebrush and the associated native grasses are fire resistant because sagebrush plants grow widely spaced, as do most of the other plants in the sagebrush community. Cheatgrass, on the other hand, is a low, fine grass that becomes extremely flammable when it cures in the early summer. Cheatgrass fires are easily started by careless people as well as lightning strikes. In even a light breeze, cheatgrass fires spread rapidly. The worst effect is that cheatgrass carries the fire to the isolated sagebrush, which burns hot. Wind-driven sage fires can generate 100-foot flame fronts moving at 50 miles per hour that burn thousands of acres in a few hours. After the fire is over, the plant that grows back first is cheatgrass, which suppresses the less flammable native grasses and makes the landscape even more fire prone. To the rancher's chagrin, cheatgrass is poor forage for cattle. Several large fire scars in the Red Rock Canyon area are directly the result of the cheatgrass invasion.

▶ **Oak Creek is named for the live oaks that grow along it. The term "live oak" means that the plant is evergreen and keeps its leaves all year. Shrub oaks often grow in thick stands with mountain mahogany and manzanita, creating formidable obstacles to cross-country hikers. However, the dense brush provides important cover for wildlife.**

Another invasive plant that has spread throughout the West and is present along stream courses in the Red Rock Canyon area is salt cedar, more commonly known as tamarisk. This tall, feathery-looking water-loving plant was introduced as a windbreak and an ornamental in the 1800s. The seeds are spread far and wide by the wind, and tamarisk takes root wherever there is enough groundwater. Although tamarisk flourishes along permanent streams and rivers, it grows along many dry washes and seasonal streams as well. Tamarisk uses

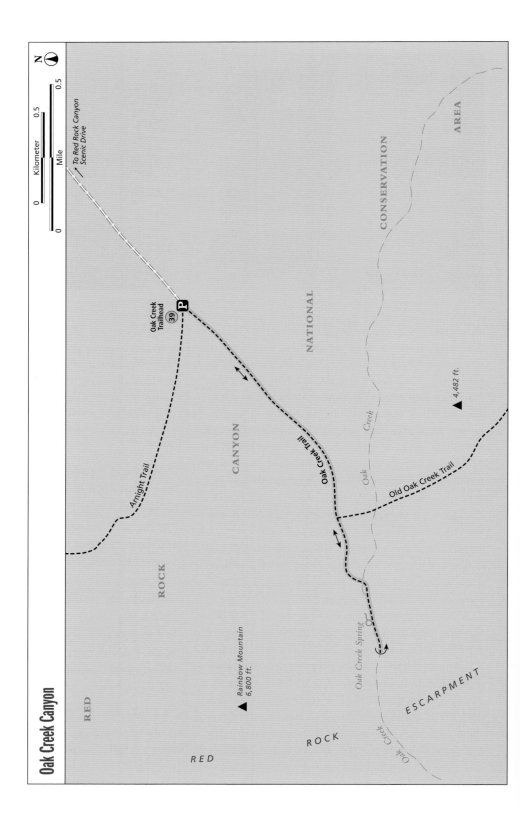

Oak Creek Canyon

RED ROCK CANYON

RED ROCK CANYON

NATIONAL CONSERVATION AREA

ESCARPMENT

▲ Rainbow Mountain
6,800 ft.

▲ 4,482 ft.

Arnight Trail

Oak Creek Trail

Old Oak Creek Trail

Oak Creek Spring

Oak Creek

Oak Creek

Oak Creek Trailhead

🅿 39

To Red Rock Canyon
Scenic Drive

N

Kilometer
0   0.5

Mile
0   0.5

a lot of water and can noticeably lower the water table and stream flows. It crowds out native species like willow and wildlife and birds that are dependent on the native vegetation. In the fall, when it has cured, the dense, feathery foliage burns easily and contributes to destructive wildfires along streams. In addition, tamarisk is extremely difficult to eradicate.

Perennial pepperweed is a weed that grows along washes and stream courses, forming a monoculture that crowds out all native plants. It increases soil salinity and provides little cover or forage for wildlife. Despite its coverage, perennial pepperweed doesn't hold soil well. It was accidentally introduced from Eurasia in the nineteenth century.

Miles and Directions

0.0 From the Oak Creek Trailhead, head southwest on the Oak Creek Trail. The Arnight Trail also leaves this trailhead to the west.

0.7 At the junction with the Old Oak Creek Trail, turn right and follow the Oak Creek Trail directly west toward the mouth of Oak Creek Canyon.

1.4 The trail ends at Oak Creek Spring; return the way you came.

2.8 Arrive back at the Oak Creek Trailhead.

40 First Creek Canyon

This is a day hike to a scenic canyon with a spring and seasonal waterfalls in the Red Rock Canyon National Conservation Area.

Start: 27.7 miles west of Las Vegas
Distance: 3.2 miles out and back
Approximate hiking time: 2 hours
Difficulty: Easy
Trail surface: Dirt and rocks
Best season: All year
Water: None
Other trail users: None
Canine compatibility: Leashed dogs permitted
Fees and permits: Entrance fee

Schedule: Open all hours
Maps: CalTopo.com MapBuilder Topo layer; USGS Blue Diamond
Trail contacts: Bureau of Land Management, Red Rock/Sloan Canyon Field Office, 1000 Scenic Loop Dr., Las Vegas 89161; (702) 515-5350; https://www.blm.gov/visit/red-rock-canyon-national-conservation-area
Special considerations: During the summer hike early in the day and carry plenty of water.

Finding the trailhead: From the intersection of US 95 and I-15 in downtown Las Vegas, drive 5.1 miles west on US 95. Exit onto Summerlin Parkway and drive 3.8 miles west. Exit onto Town Center Drive and turn left. Continue 2.3 miles, and then turn right onto West Charleston Boulevard, NV 159. Continue 10.3 miles to the First Creek Trailhead, on the right. GPS: N36 4.904'/W115 26.881'

The Hike

The trail to First Creek Canyon heads directly west toward the obvious mouth of First Creek Canyon. The first section of the trail is fenced off to help the surrounding desert regenerate; please respect this closure. As the trail approaches the mouth of the canyon, you'll encounter a few ponderosa pines, growing in this unusual location because of the cooler air draining out of First Creek Canyon. Deciduous trees mark First Creek Spring and the end of the hike. Return the way you came.

Ironically, someone manages to drown in the desert every year. Usually they are the victims of flash flooding. In sandstone canyon country, three factors combine to make flash floods common. One is the occurrence of sudden heavy rain, primarily during the later summer thunderstorm season. The second is the large expanses of bare rock and sparsely vegetated soil that are typical of desert landscapes. And the third is the existence of long, narrow canyons such as First Creek Canyon and the other canyons cutting into the Red Rock Escarpment.

Thunderstorms in this area are capable of producing rainfall rates in excess of 3 inches per hour. Imagine a sheet of water 3 inches thick draped across several square miles of land and bare rock, and you realize just how much water that is. Since there is little vegetation to retain the runoff and help it soak into the ground, the runoff rapidly fills drainages and gathers in the canyons. As tributaries combine into larger canyons, the flood gets deeper. In the lower reaches of a canyon, the flow will increase suddenly and dramatically. How fast the water rises depends on the size of the flood and the shape of the canyon. Very narrow canyons tend to flood very abruptly, and often the only warning is a freight-train roar. If a hiker doesn't have a place to escape to high ground immediately, the outcome is usually fatal.

A lot of people envision a flash flood as a wall of water that immediately overwhelms everything in its path. While such flash floods do occur, more commonly the flow starts to increase and the water turns muddy, or a dry wash starts to run. The flood may only be a couple of feet deep, but it just takes a foot of fast moving water to sweep a person off his feet and drown him.

Joshua trees are found on the desert slopes below the Red Rock Escarpment.

The danger of flash floods is not so much the "wall of water" effect as that the flow may rapidly increase without warning. Flash floods can travel many miles downstream from the headwaters where the rain fell, and at your location there may be no sign of rain or bad weather.

Drivers often drown when trying to cross a flooded desert wash on a desert road, not realizing that the road bed may be washed away and the water is much deeper than it appears. A foot or two of swift floodwater is enough to sweep away and roll even a pickup truck or SUV. If you are stranded in a flooding wash in your vehicle, stay with it if possible, and don't try to wade or swim to shore.

Another common mistake is to camp or park in a dry wash. Because the storm that causes the flood may be so far away, there's no warning until the water starts to rise.

▶ Springs such as First Creek and Oak Creek are commonly located at the mouths of canyons in Nevada's Basin and Range country. The reason for this is that the mountain escarpment is generally located along a fault line, where the mountain was lifted upward relative to the adjacent valley. This movement causes the rocks to fracture, and water often rises from the aquifer below to the surface along the fault line.

First Creek Canyon

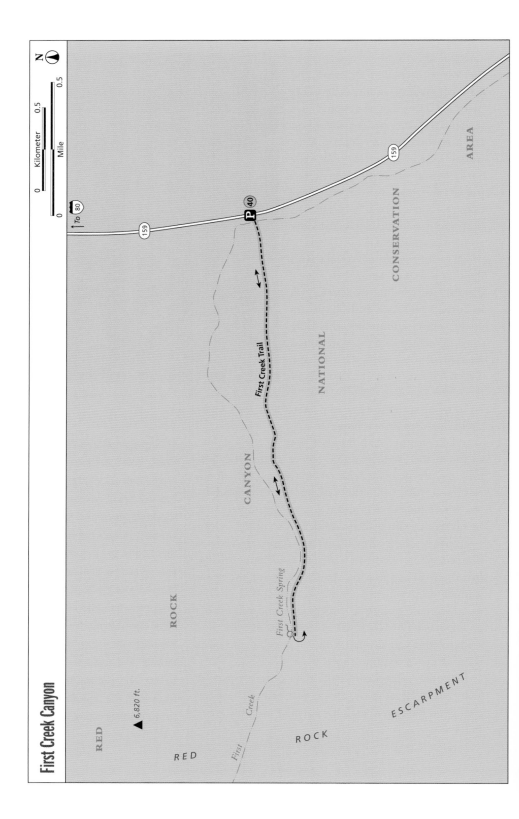

RED ROCK

▲ 6,820 ft.

RED ROCK ESCARPMENT

First Creek

CANYON

First Creek Spring

First Creek Trail

NATIONAL

CONSERVATION AREA

P 40

159

159

To 80

N

Kilometer
0   0.5

Mile
0   0.5

Though winter storms typically produce gentle rainfall, sometimes large amounts of tropical moisture, often the remnants of a hurricane, are drawn up into southern Nevada and trigger prolonged rains. Once the ground becomes saturated, drainages and canyons may start to flood. These floods may last for days, and frustrated hikers or drivers may try to cross flooded washes, with deadly consequences.

Miles and Directions

0.0 Leave the First Creek Trailhead on the First Creek Trail.

1.6 Arrive at First Creek Spring in the mouth of First Creek Canyon; return the way you came.

3.2 Arrive back at First Creek Trailhead.

The Art of Hiking

When standing nose to nose with a mountain lion, you're probably not too concerned with the issue of ethical behavior in the wild. No doubt you're just terrified. But let's be honest. How often are you nose to nose with a mountain lion? For most of us, a hike into the "wild" means loading up the SUV with expensive gear and driving to a toileted trailhead. Sure, you can mourn how civilized we've become—how GPS units have replaced natural instinct and Gore-Tex stands in for true grit—but the silly gadgets of civilization aside, we have plenty of reason to take pride in how we've matured. With survival now on the back burner, we've begun to understand that we have a responsibility to protect, no longer just conquer, our wild places: that they, not we, are at risk. So please, do what you can. The following section will help you understand better what it means to "do what you can" while still making the most of your hiking experience. Anyone can take a hike, but hiking safely and well is an art requiring preparation and proper equipment.

Trail Etiquette

Leave no trace. Always leave an area just like you found it—if not better than you found it. Avoid camping in fragile, alpine meadows and along the banks of streams and lakes. Use a camp stove versus building a wood fire. (All of the areas in this book prohibit backcountry campfires.) Pack up all of your trash and extra food. Bury human waste at least 100 feet from open water and dry desert washes under 6 to 8 inches of topsoil. Don't bathe with soap in a lake or stream—use prepackaged moistened towels to wipe off sweat and dirt, or bathe in the water without soap.

Stay on the trail. It's true, a path anywhere leads nowhere new, but purists will just have to get over it. Paths serve an important purpose; they limit impact on natural areas. Straying from a designated trail may seem innocent, but it can cause damage to sensitive areas—damage that may take years to recover, if it can recover at all. Even simple shortcuts can be destructive. So, please, stay on the trail, whether officially constructed or made by hikers.

Leave no weeds. Noxious weeds tend to overtake other plants, which in turn affects animals and birds that depend on them for food. To minimize the spread of noxious weeds, hikers should regularly clean their boots, tents, packs, and hiking poles of mud and seeds. Also brush your dog to remove any weed seeds before heading off into a new area.

Keep your dog under control. You can buy a flexi-lead that allows your dog to go exploring along the trail, while allowing you the ability to reel him in should another hiker approach or should he decide to chase a rabbit. (But remember that Valley of Fire State Park limits leashes to 6 feet.) Always obey leash laws, and be sure to bury your dog's waste or pack it out in resealable plastic bags.

Respect other trail users. Often you're not the only one on the trail. With the rise in popularity of multiuse trails, you'll have to learn a new kind of respect, beyond the nod and "hello" approach you may be used to. First investigate whether you're on a multiuse trail, and assume the appropriate precautions. When you encounter motorized vehicles (ATVs, motorcycles, and 4WDs), be alert. Though they should always yield to the hiker, often they're going too fast or are too lost in the buzz of their engine to react to your presence. If you hear activity ahead, step off the trail just to be safe. Note that you're not likely to hear a mountain biker coming, so be prepared and know ahead of time whether you share the trail with them. Cyclists should always yield to hikers, but that's little comfort to the hiker. Be aware. When you approach horses or pack animals on the trail, always step quietly off the trail, preferably on the downhill side, and let them pass. If you're wearing a large backpack, it's often a good idea to sit down. To some animals, a hiker wearing a large backpack might appear threatening. Many national forests allow domesticated grazing, usually for sheep and cattle. Make sure your dog doesn't harass these animals, and respect ranchers' rights while you're enjoying yours.

Getting into Shape

Unless you want to be sore—and possibly have to shorten your trip or vacation—be sure to get in shape before a big hike. If you're terribly out of shape, start a walking program early, preferably eight weeks in advance. Start with a fifteen-minute walk during your lunch hour or after work and gradually increase your walking time to an hour. You should also increase your elevation gain. Walking briskly up hills really strengthens your leg muscles and gets your heart rate up. If you work in a storied office building, take the stairs instead of the elevator. If you prefer going to a gym, walk the treadmill or use a stair machine. You can further increase your strength and endurance by walking with a loaded backpack. Stationary exercises you might consider are squats, leg lifts, sit-ups, and push-ups. Other good ways to get in shape include biking, running, aerobics, and, of course, short hikes. Stretching before and after a hike keeps muscles flexible and helps avoid injuries.

Preparedness

It's been said that failing to plan means planning to fail. So do take the necessary time to plan your trip. Whether going on a short day hike or an extended backpack trip, always prepare for the worst. Simply remembering to pack a copy of the *U.S. Army Survival Manual* is not preparedness. Although it's not a bad idea if you plan on entering truly wild places, it's merely the tourniquet answer to a problem. You need to do your best to prevent the problem from arising in the first place. In order to survive—and to stay reasonably comfortable—you need to concern yourself with the basics: water, food, and shelter. Don't go on a hike without having these bases covered. And don't go on a hike expecting to find these items in the woods.

Water. Even in frigid conditions, you need at least two quarts of water a day to function efficiently. Add heat and taxing terrain and you can bump that figure up to two gallons. That's simply a base to work from—your metabolism and your level of conditioning can raise or lower that amount. Unless you know your level, assume that you need one gallon of water a day. Now, where do you plan on getting the water?

Preferably not from natural water sources. These sources can be loaded with intestinal disturbers, such as bacteria, viruses, and fertilizers. *Giardia lamblia,* the most common of these disturbers, is a protozoan parasite that lives part of its life cycle as a cyst in water sources. The parasite spreads when mammals defecate in water sources. Once ingested, giardia can induce cramping, diarrhea, vomiting, and fatigue within two days to two weeks after ingestion. Giardiasis is treatable with prescription drugs. If you believe you've contracted giardiasis, see a doctor immediately.

Treating water. The best and easiest solution to avoid polluted water is to carry your water with you. Yet, depending on the nature of your hike and the duration, this may not be an option—one gallon of water weighs eight and a half pounds. In that case, you'll need to look into treating water. Regardless of which method you choose, you should always carry some water with you in case of an emergency. Save this reserve until you absolutely need it.

There are three methods of treating water: boiling, chemical treatment, and filtering. If you boil water, current studies show that bringing water to a boil—at any altitude—is sufficient to kill all disease organisms. After boiling, remove the flat taste by pouring the water back and forth between two containers several times. You can opt for chlorine dioxide tablet or iodine chemical treatment, which will kill all dangerous organisms but will not take care of chemical pollutants. Another drawback to chemical treatments is the unpleasant taste of the water after it's treated. You can remedy this by adding powdered drink mix to the water. Filters do not remove viruses such as hepatitis unless they are labeled as water purifiers, but they do remove giardia and organic and inorganic contaminants, and they don't leave an aftertaste. Water filters are far from perfect, as they can easily become clogged or leak if a gasket wears out. It's always a good idea to carry a backup supply of chemical treatment tablets in case your filter decides to quit on you.

Food. If we're talking about survival, you can go days without food, as long as you have water. But we're also talking about comfort. Try to avoid foods that are high in sugar and fat like candy bars and potato chips. These food types are harder to digest and are low in nutritional value. Instead, bring along foods that are easy to pack, nutritious, and high in energy (e.g., bagels, nutrition bars, dehydrated fruit, gorp, and jerky). If you are on an overnight trip, easy-to-fix dinners include rice mixes with dehydrated potatoes, corn, pasta with cheese sauce, and soup mixes. For a tasty breakfast, you can fix hot oatmeal with brown sugar and reconstituted milk powder topped off with banana chips. If you like a hot drink in the morning, bring along herbal tea bags or hot chocolate. If you are a coffee junkie, you can purchase coffee that is packaged like tea bags. You can prepackage all of your meals in heavy-duty resealable plastic bags to keep food from spilling in your pack. These bags can be reused to pack out trash.

Shelter. The type of shelter you choose depends less on the conditions than on your tolerance for discomfort. Shelter comes in many forms—tent, tarp, lean-to, bivy sack, cabin, cave, etc. If you're camping in the desert, a bivy sack may suffice, but if you're above the tree line and a storm is approaching, a better choice is a three- or four-season tent. Tents are the logical and most popular choice for most backpackers, as they're lightweight and packable—and you can rest assured that you always have shelter from the elements. Before you leave on your trip, anticipate what the weather and terrain will be like, and plan for the type of shelter that will work best for your comfort level (see "Equipment" later in this section).

Finding a campsite. If there are established campsites, stick to those. If not, start looking for a campsite early—around 3:30 or 4:00 p.m. Stop at the first decent site you see. Depending on the area, it could be a long time before you find another suitable location. Pitch your camp in an area that's level. Make sure the area is at least 200 feet from fragile areas like lakeshores, meadows, and stream banks. And try to avoid areas thick in underbrush, as they can harbor insects and provide cover for approaching animals.

If you are camping in stormy, rainy weather, look for a rock outcrop or a shelter in the trees to keep the wind from blowing your tent all night. Be sure that you don't camp under trees with dead limbs that might break off on top of you. Also, try to find an area that has an absorbent surface, such as sandy soil or forest duff. This, in addition to camping on a surface with a slight angle, will provide better drainage. By all means, don't dig trenches to provide drainage around your tent—remember you're practicing zero-impact camping.

If you're in bear country, steer clear of creekbeds or animal paths. If you see any signs of a bear's presence (i.e., scat, footprints), relocate. You'll need to find a campsite near a tall tree where you can hang your food and other items that may attract bears, such as deodorant, toothpaste, or soap. Carry a lightweight nylon rope with which to hang your food. As a rule, you should hang your food at least 20 feet from the ground and 5 feet away from the tree trunk. You can put food and other items in a waterproof stuff sack and tie one end of the rope to the stuff sack. To get the other end of the rope over the tree branch, tie a good size rock to it, and gently toss the rock over the tree branch. Pull the stuff sack up until it reaches the top of the branch and tie it off securely. Don't hang your food near your tent! If possible, hang your food at least 100 feet away from your campsite. Alternatives to hanging your food are bear-proof plastic tubes and metal bear boxes.

Lastly, think of comfort. Lie down on the ground where you intend to sleep and see if it's a good fit. For morning warmth (and a nice view to wake up to), have your tent face east.

I know you're tough, but get 10 miles into the woods and develop a blister and you'll wish you had carried that first-aid kit. Face it, it's just plain good sense. Many companies produce lightweight, compact first-aid kits. Just make sure yours contains at least the following:

- adhesive bandages
- moleskin or duct tape
- various sterile gauze and dressings
- white surgical tape
- an Ace bandage
- an antihistamine
- aspirin
- Betadine solution
- a first-aid book
- antacid tablets
- tweezers
- scissors
- antibacterial wipes
- triple-antibiotic ointment
- plastic gloves
- sterile cotton tip applicators
- syrup of ipecac (to induce vomiting)
- thermometer
- wire splint

Here are a few tips for dealing with and hopefully preventing certain ailments.

Sunburn. Take along sunscreen or sunblock, protective clothing, and a wide-brimmed hat. If you do get a sunburn, treat the area with aloe vera gel, and protect the area from further sun exposure. At higher elevations, the sun's radiation can be particularly damaging to skin. Remember that your eyes are vulnerable to this radiation as well. Sunglasses can be a good way to prevent headaches and permanent eye damage from the sun, especially in places where light-colored rock or patches of snow reflect light up in your face. They should be considered essential in southern Nevada during the spring and summer.

Blisters. Be prepared to take care of these hike-spoilers by carrying moleskin (a lightly padded adhesive), gauze and tape, or adhesive bandages. An effective way to apply moleskin is to cut out a circle of moleskin and remove the center—like a doughnut—and place it over the blistered area. Cutting the center out will reduce the pressure applied to the sensitive skin. Other products can help you combat blisters. Some are applied to suspicious hot spots before a blister forms to help decrease friction to that area, while others are applied to the blister after it has popped to help prevent further irritation.

Insect bites and stings. You can treat most insect bites and stings by applying hydrocortisone 1 percent cream topically and taking ibuprofen to reduce inflammation and swelling. If you forgot to pack these items, a cold compress or a paste of mud and ashes can sometimes assuage the itching and discomfort. Remove any stingers by using tweezers or scraping the area with your fingernail or a knife blade. Don't pinch the area, as you'll only spread the venom.

Some hikers are highly sensitive to bites and stings and may have a serious allergic reaction that can be life-threatening. Symptoms of a serious allergic reaction can include wheezing, an asthmatic attack, and shock. The treatment for this severe type of reaction is epinephrine. If you know that you are sensitive to bites and stings, carry a prepackaged kit of epinephrine, which can be obtained from a pharmacist.

Ticks. Ticks can carry diseases such as Rocky Mountain spotted fever and Lyme disease. The best defense is, of course, prevention. If you know you're going to be hiking through an area littered with ticks, wear long pants and a long-sleeved shirt. You can apply a permethrin repellent to your clothing and a DEET repellent to exposed skin. At the end of your hike, do a spot check for ticks (and insects). If you do find a tick, grab the head of the tick firmly—with a pair of tweezers if you have them—and gently pull it away from the skin with a twisting motion. Sometimes the mouth parts linger, embedded in your skin. If this happens, try to remove them with a disinfected needle. Clean the affected area with an antibacterial cleanser and then apply triple antibiotic ointment. Monitor the area for a few days. If irritation persists or a white spot develops, see a doctor for possible infection.

Poison ivy, oak, and sumac. These skin irritants can be found most anywhere in North America and come in the form of a bush or a vine, having leaflets in groups of three, five, seven, or nine. Learn how to spot the plants. The oil they secrete can cause an allergic reaction in the form of blisters, usually about twelve hours after exposure. The itchy rash can last from ten days to several weeks. The best defense against these irritants is to wear clothing that covers the arms, legs, and torso. For summer, zip-off cargo pants come in handy. There are also nonprescription lotions you can apply to exposed skin that guard against the effects of poison ivy/oak/sumac and can be washed off with soap and water. If you think you were in contact with the plants, after hiking (or even on the trail during longer hikes) wash with soap and water. Taking a hot shower with soap after you return home from your hike will also help to remove any lingering oil from your skin. Should you contract a rash from any of these plants, use an antihistamine to reduce the itching. If the rash is localized, create a light bleach/water wash to dry up the area. If the rash has spread, either tough it out or see your doctor about getting a dose of cortisone (available both orally and by injection).

Snakebites. Snakebites are rare in North America. Unless startled or provoked, the majority of snakes will not bite. If you are wise to their habitats and keep a careful eye on the trail, you should be just fine. When stepping over logs, first step on the log, making sure you can see what's on the other side before stepping down. Though your chances of being struck are slim, it's wise to know what to do in the event you are.

If a *nonvenomous* snake bites you, allow the wound to bleed a small amount and then cleanse the wounded area with a Betadine solution (10 percent povidone iodine). Rinse the wound with clean water (preferably) or fresh urine (it might sound ugly, but it's sterile). Once the area is clean, cover it with triple antibiotic ointment and a clean bandage. Remember, most residual damage from snakebites, venomous or otherwise, comes from infection, not the snake's venom. Keep the area as clean as possible and get medical attention immediately.

If somebody in your party is bitten by a venomous snake, follow these steps:

1. Calm the patient.

2. Remove jewelry, watches, and restrictive clothing, and immobilize the affected limb. Do not elevate the injury. Medical opinions vary on whether the area should be lower or level with the heart, but the consensus is that it should not be above it.

3. Make a note of the circumference of the limb at the bite site and at various points above the site as well. This will help you monitor swelling.

4. Evacuate your victim. Ideally he should be carried out to minimize movement. If the victim appears to be doing okay, he can walk. Stop and rest frequently, and if the swelling appears to be spreading or the patient's symptoms increase, change your plan and find a way to get your patient transported.

5. If you are waiting for rescue, make sure to keep your patient comfortable and hydrated (unless he begins vomiting).

Snakebite treatment is rife with old-fashioned remedies: You used to be told to cut and suck the venom out of the bite site or to use a suction cup extractor for the same purpose; applying an electric shock to the area was even in vogue for a while. Do not do any of these things. Do not apply ice, do not give your patient painkillers, and do not apply a tourniquet. All you really want to do is keep your patient calm and get help. If you're alone and have to hike out, don't run—you'll only increase the flow of blood and venom throughout your system. Instead, walk calmly. Rattlesnake bites are very rarely fatal.

Dehydration. Have you ever hiked in hot weather and had a roaring headache and felt fatigued after only a few miles? More than likely you were dehydrated. Symptoms of dehydration include fatigue, headache, and decreased coordination and judgment. When you are hiking, your body's rate of fluid loss depends on the outside temperature, humidity, altitude, and your activity level. On average, a hiker walking in warm weather will lose four liters of fluid a day. That fluid loss is easily replaced by normal consumption of liquids and food. However, if a hiker is walking briskly in hot, dry weather in the desert, he or she can lose one to three liters of water an hour. It's important to always carry plenty of water and to stop often and drink fluids regularly, even if you aren't thirsty.

Heat exhaustion is the result of a loss of large amounts of electrolytes and often occurs if a hiker is dehydrated and has been under heavy exertion. Common symptoms of heat exhaustion include cramping, exhaustion, fatigue, lightheadedness, and nausea. You can treat heat exhaustion by getting out of the sun and drinking an electrolyte solution made up of one teaspoon of salt and one tablespoon of sugar dissolved in a liter of water. Drink this solution slowly over a period of one hour. Drinking plenty of fluids (preferably an electrolyte solution/sports drink) can prevent heat exhaustion. Avoid hiking during the hottest parts of the day, and wear breathable clothing, a wide-brimmed hat, and sunglasses.

Hypothermia is one of the biggest dangers in the backcountry, especially for day hikers in the summertime. That may sound strange, but imagine starting out on a hike in midsummer when it's sunny and 80 degrees out. You're clad in nylon shorts and a cotton T-shirt. About halfway through your hike, the sky begins to cloud up, and in the next hour a light drizzle begins to fall and the wind starts to pick up. Before you know it, you are soaking wet and shivering—the perfect recipe for hypothermia. More advanced signs include decreased coordination, slurred speech, and blurred vision. When a victim's temperature falls below 92 degrees, the blood pressure and pulse plummet, possibly leading to coma and death.

To avoid hypothermia, always bring a windproof/rainproof shell, a fleece jacket, long underwear made of a breathable, synthetic fiber, gloves, and hat when you are hiking in the mountains. Learn to adjust your clothing layers based on the temperature. If you are climbing uphill at a moderate pace you will stay warm, but when you stop for a break you'll become cold quickly, unless you add more layers of clothing.

If a hiker is showing advanced signs of hypothermia, dress him or her in dry clothes and make sure he or she is wearing a hat and gloves. Place the person in a sleeping bag in a tent or shelter that will protect him or her from the wind and other elements. Give the person warm fluids to drink and keep him awake.

Frostbite. When the mercury dips below 32 degrees, your extremities begin to chill. If a persistent chill attacks a localized area, say, your hands or your toes, the circulatory system reacts by cutting off blood flow to the affected area—the idea being to protect and preserve the body's overall temperature. And so it's death by attrition for the affected area. Ice crystals start to form from the water in the cells of the neglected tissue. Deprived of heat, nourishment, and now water, the tissue literally starves. This is frostbite.

Prevention is your best defense against this situation. Most prone to frostbite are your face, hands, and feet, so protect these areas well. Wool is the traditional material of choice because it provides ample air space for insulation and draws moisture away from the skin. Synthetic fabrics, however, have made great strides in the cold weather clothing market. Do your research. A pair of light silk liners under your regular gloves is a good trick for keeping warm. They afford some additional warmth, but, more important, they'll allow you to remove your mitts for detail work without exposing the skin.

If your feet or hands start to feel cold or numb due to the elements, warm them as quickly as possible. Place cold hands under your armpits or bury them in your crotch. If your feet are cold, change your socks. If there's plenty of room in your boots, add another pair of socks. Do remember, though, that constricting your feet in tight boots can restrict blood flow and actually make your feet colder more quickly. Your socks need to have breathing room if they're going to be effective. Dead air provides insulation. If your face is cold, place your warm hands over your face, or simply wear a head stocking.

Should your skin go numb and start to appear white and waxy, chances are you've got or are developing frostbite. Don't try to thaw the area unless you can maintain the warmth. In other words, don't stop to warm up your frostbitten feet only to head back on the trail. You'll do more damage than good. Tests have shown that hikers who walked on thawed feet did more harm, and endured more pain, than hikers who left the affected areas alone. Do your best to get out of the cold entirely and seek medical attention—which usually consists of performing a rapid rewarming in water for twenty to thirty minutes.

The overall objective in preventing both hypothermia and frostbite is to keep the body's core warm. Protect key areas where heat escapes, like the top of the head, and maintain the proper nutrition level. Foods that are high in calories aid the body in producing heat. Never smoke or drink when you're in situations where the cold is threatening. By affecting blood flow, these activities ultimately cool the body's core temperature.

Altitude sickness (AMS). High lofty peaks, clear alpine lakes, and vast mountain views beckon hikers to the high country. But those who like to venture high may become victims of altitude sickness (also known as acute mountain sickness—AMS). Altitude sickness is your body's reaction to insufficient oxygen in the blood due to decreased barometric pressure. While some hikers may feel lightheaded, nauseous, and experience shortness of breath at 7,000 feet, others may not experience these symptoms until they reach 10,000 feet or higher.

Slowing your ascent to high places and giving your body a chance to acclimatize to the higher elevations can prevent altitude sickness. For example, if you live at sea level and are planning a weeklong backpacking trip to elevations between 7,000 and 12,000 feet, start by staying below 7,000 feet for one night, then move to between 7,000 and 10,000 feet for another night or two. Avoid strenuous exertion and alcohol to give your body a chance to adjust to the new altitude. It's also important to eat light food and drink plenty of nonalcoholic fluids, preferably water. Loss of appetite at altitude is common, but you must eat!

Most hikers who experience mild to moderate AMS develop a headache and/or nausea, grow lethargic, and have problems sleeping. The treatment for AMS is simple: Stop heading uphill. Keep eating and drinking water, and take meds for the headache. You actually need to take more breaths at altitude than at sea level, so breathe a little faster without hyperventilating. If symptoms don't improve over twenty-four to forty-eight hours, descend. Once a victim descends about 2,000 to 3,000 feet, his signs will usually begin to diminish.

Severe AMS comes in two forms: high altitude pulmonary edema (HAPE) and high altitude cerebral edema (HACE). HAPE, an accumulation of fluid in the lungs, can occur above 8,000 feet. Symptoms include rapid heart rate, shortness of breath at rest, AMS symptoms, dry cough developing into a wet cough, gurgling sounds, flu-like or bronchitis symptoms, and lack of muscle coordination. HAPE is life-threatening, so descend immediately, at least 2,000 to 4,000 feet. HACE usually occurs above 12,000 feet but sometimes occurs above 10,000 feet. Symptoms are similar to HAPE but also include seizures, hallucinations, paralysis, and vision disturbances. Descend immediately—HACE is also life-threatening.

Hantavirus pulmonary syndrome (HPS). Deer mice spread the virus that causes HPS, and humans contract it from breathing it in, usually when they've disturbed an area with dust and mice feces from nests or surfaces with mice droppings or urine. Exposure to large numbers of rodents and their feces or urine presents the greatest risk. As hikers, we sometimes enter old buildings, and often deer mice live in these places. We may not be around long enough to be exposed, but do be aware of this disease. About half the people who develop HPS die. Symptoms are flu-like and appear about two to three weeks after exposure. After initial symptoms, a dry cough and shortness of breath follow. Breathing is difficult. If you even think you might have HPS, see a doctor immediately!

Natural Hazards

Besides tripping over a rock or tree root on the trail, there are some real hazards to be aware of while hiking. Even if where you're hiking doesn't have the plethora of venomous snakes, toxic plants, insects, and grizzly bears found in other parts of the United States, there are a few weather conditions and predators you may need to take into account.

Lightning. Thunderstorms build over the mountains almost every day during the summer. Lightning is generated by thunderheads and can strike without warning, even several miles away from the nearest overhead cloud. The best rule of thumb is to start leaving exposed peaks, ridges, and canyon rims by about noon. This time can vary a little depending on storm buildup. Keep an eye on cloud formation, and don't underestimate how fast a storm can build. The bigger they get, the more likely a thunderstorm will happen. Lightning takes the path of least resistance, so if you're the high point, it might choose you. Ducking under a rock overhang is dangerous, as you form the shortest path between the rock and ground. If you dash below tree line, avoid standing under the only or the tallest tree. If you are caught above tree line, stay away from anything metal you might be carrying. Move down off the ridge slightly to a low, treeless point and squat until the storm passes. If you have an insulating pad, squat on it. Avoid having both your hands and feet touching the ground at once, and never lie flat. If you hear a buzzing sound or feel your hair standing on end, move quickly, as an electrical charge is building up.

Flash floods. On July 31, 1976, a torrential downpour unleashed by a thunderstorm dumped tons of water into the Big Thompson watershed near Estes Park. Within hours, a wall of water moved down the narrow canyon killing 139 people and causing more than $30 million in property damage. The spooky thing about flash floods, especially in western canyons, is that they can appear out of nowhere from a storm many miles away. While hiking or driving in canyons, keep an eye on the weather. Always climb to safety if danger threatens. Flash floods usually subside quickly, so be patient, and don't cross a swollen stream.

Bears. Most of the United States (outside of the Pacific Northwest and parts of the Northern Rockies) does not have a grizzly bear population, although some rumors exist about sightings where there should be none. Black bears are plentiful, however. Here are some tips in case you and a bear scare each other. Most of all, avoid surprising a bear. Talk or sing where visibility or hearing is limited, such as along a rushing creek or in thick brush. In grizzly country especially, carry bear spray in a holster on your pack belt where you can quickly grab it. While hiking, watch for bear tracks (five toes), droppings (sizable with leaves, partly digested berries, seeds, and/or animal fur), or rocks and roots along the trail that show signs of being dug up (this could be a bear looking for bugs to eat). Keep a clean camp, hang food or use bearproof storage containers, and don't sleep in the clothes you wore while cooking. Be especially careful to avoid getting between a mother and her cubs. In late summer and fall, bears are busy eating to fatten up for winter, so be extra careful around berry bushes and oak brush. If you do encounter a bear, move away slowly while facing the bear, talk softly, and avoid direct eye contact. Give the bear room to escape. Since bears are very curious, it might stand upright to get a better whiff of you, and it may even charge you to try to intimidate you. Try to stay calm. If a black bear attacks you, fight back with anything you have handy. If a grizzly bear attacks you, your best option is to "play dead" by lying facedown on the ground and covering the back of your neck and head with your hands. Unleashed dogs have been known to come running back to their owners with a bear close behind. Keep your dog on a leash or leave it at home.

Mountain lions appear to be getting more comfortable around humans as long as deer (their favorite prey) are in an area with adequate cover. Usually elusive and quiet, lions rarely attack people. If you meet a lion, give it a chance to escape. Stay calm and talk firmly to it. Back away slowly while facing the lion. If you run, you'll only encourage the cat to chase you. Make yourself look large by opening a jacket, if you have one, or waving your hiking poles. If the lion behaves aggressively throw stones, sticks, or whatever you can while remaining tall. If a lion does attack, fight for your life with anything you can grab.

Africanized bees have spread into the desert Southwest. Although their sting is no worse than that of a European honeybee, Africanized bees are much more aggressive. When hiking, avoid all bees and especially any that are swarming. Avoid anything that is scented, including scented soap, shampoo, hair spray, perfumes and colognes, and chewing gum. If you're hiking with a dog, keep it on a leash and do not let it roam through brush. Dogs have triggered a number of attacks.

If attacked, seek the shelter of a vehicle or building if available. In the backcountry, run and keep running. Africanized bees commonly pursue for a quarter to a half mile. Don't fight or flail at the bees—the scent of crushed bees further incites their attack. Africanized bees go for your head and face, so cover your head with loose clothing and protect your face. Run through brush or dense foliage if it is handy—dense vegetation confuses bees.

Hunting is a popular sport in the United States, especially during rifle season in October and November. Hiking is still enjoyable in those months in many areas, so just take a few precautions. First, learn when the different hunting seasons start and end in the area in which you'll be hiking. During this time frame, be sure to wear at least a blaze orange hat, and possibly put an orange vest over your pack. Don't be surprised to see hunters in camo outfits carrying bows or rifles around during their season. If you would feel more comfortable without hunters around, hike in national parks and monuments or state and local parks where hunting is not allowed.

Navigation

Whether you are going on a short hike in a familiar area or planning a weeklong backpack trip, you should always be equipped with the proper navigational equipment—at the very least a detailed map and a sturdy compass.

Maps. There are many different types of maps available to help you find your way on the trail. Easiest to find are USDA Forest Service maps and BLM (Bureau of Land Management) maps. These maps tend to cover large areas, so be sure they are detailed enough for your particular trip. You can also obtain national park maps as well as high quality maps from private companies and trail groups. These maps can be obtained either from outdoor stores or ranger stations.

US Geological Survey topographic maps are particularly popular with hikers—especially serious backcountry hikers. These maps contain the standard map symbols such as roads, lakes, and rivers, as well as contour lines that accurately show the details of the trail terrain like ridges, valleys, passes, and mountain peaks. The 7.5-minute series (1 inch on the map equals approximately ⅖ mile on the ground) provides the closest inspection available. USGS maps are available from https://ngmdb.usgs.gov/topoview; you can download maps for free or order printed copies.

Computer-based digital maps have significant advantages over traditional maps. Services such as GaiaGPS.com and CalTopo.com are web-based and also available on phone apps. Basic mapping is available for free, and advanced features are available with a paid subscription. You can view and overlay many different map layers, including USGS 7.5-minute topo maps, satellite and aerial images, wildfire history, and many more. Mapping tools allow you to plan your hike, noting distances and elevation changes. And you can print a copy of your custom map for your hike—always a good idea in case your electronic maps fail.

The art of map reading is a skill that you can develop by first practicing in an area you are familiar with. To begin, orient the map so the map is lined up in the correct direction (i.e., north on the map is lined up with true north). Next, familiarize yourself with the map symbols and try and match them up with terrain features around you such as a high ridge, mountain peak, river, or lake. If you are practicing with a topographic map, notice the contour lines. On gentler terrain these contour lines are spaced farther apart, and on steeper terrain they are closer together. Pick a short loop trail, and stop frequently to check your position on the map. As you practice map reading, you'll learn how to anticipate a steep section on the trail or a good place to take a rest break, and so on.

Compasses. First off, the sun is not a substitute for a compass. So, what kind of compass should you have? Here are some characteristics you should look for: an orienteering-type compass, which has a rectangular base with detailed scales, a liquid-filled housing, protective housing, a sighting line on the mirror, luminous alignment and back-bearing arrows, a luminous north-seeking arrow, and a well-defined bezel ring.

You can learn compass basics by reading the detailed instructions included with your compass. If you want to fine-tune your compass skills, sign up for an orienteering class or purchase a book on compass reading. Once you've learned the basic skills of using a compass, remember to practice these skills before you head into the backcountry.

GPS (Global Positioning System). Once you have learned basic compass skills, you may be interested in checking out the technical wizardry of the GPS device. The GPS was developed by the US Department of Defense and works off twenty-four NAVSTAR satellites orbiting 12,000 miles above the Earth. A trail GPS receiver is a handheld unit that continuously calculates your latitude and longitude. GPS units, even on smartphones, provide nearly pinpoint accuracy, within 16 feet or so—which is more accurate than the best topographic maps.

There are many different types of GPS units available, and they range in price from $100 to $600. In general, all GPS units have a display screen and keypad where you input information. All units allow you to plot your route, easily retrace your path, track your traveling speed, find the mileage between waypoints, and calculate the total mileage of your route. Better units have built-in or downloadable topographic maps showing roads and trails. They also receive the Russian GLONASS and European Galileo satellites, further increasing accuracy and the likelihood of maintaining a position fix where the view of the sky is limited.

Before you purchase a GPS unit, keep in mind that these devices may have difficulty picking up signals indoors, in heavily wooded areas, or in narrow canyons. Also, batteries can wear out or other technical problems can develop. A GPS unit should be always used in conjunction with a map and compass, not in place of those items.

Pedometers. A pedometer is a small, clip-on unit with a digital display that calculates your hiking distance in miles or kilometers based on your walking stride. Some units also calculate the calories you burn and your total hiking time. Pedometers are available at most large outdoor stores and range in price from $20 to $40. There are also pedometer apps for phones, as well as fitness watches that track not only distance and time but also heart rate and other parameters.

Trip Planning

Planning your hiking adventure begins with letting a friend or relative know your trip itinerary so they can call for help if you don't return at your scheduled time. Your next task is to make sure you are outfitted to experience the risks and rewards of the trail. This section highlights gear and clothing you may want to take with you to get the most out of your hike.

Day Hikes

- ❑ camera
- ❑ printed map
- ❑ compass
- ❑ GPS unit
- ❑ pedometer
- ❑ daypack
- ❑ first-aid kit
- ❑ food
- ❑ guidebook
- ❑ LED headlamp/flashlight with extra batteries and bulbs
- ❑ hat
- ❑ insect repellent
- ❑ knife/multipurpose tool
- ❑ map
- ❑ matches in waterproof container and fire starter
- ❑ fleece jacket
- ❑ rain gear
- ❑ space blanket
- ❑ sunglasses
- ❑ sunscreen

- ❑ swimsuit and/or fishing gear (if hiking to a lake or swimming hole)
- ❑ watch
- ❑ water
- ❑ water bottles/water hydration system

Overnight Trip

- ❑ backpack and waterproof rain cover
- ❑ backpacker's trowel
- ❑ bandanna
- ❑ biodegradable soap
- ❑ pot scrubber
- ❑ multiple collapsible water containers (1 or 2 quarts each)
- ❑ clothing—extra wool socks, shirt and shorts
- ❑ cook set/utensils
- ❑ ditty bags to store gear
- ❑ extra plastic resealable bags
- ❑ gaiters
- ❑ garbage bag
- ❑ ground cloth
- ❑ journal/pen
- ❑ nylon rope to hang food
- ❑ long underwear
- ❑ permit (if required)
- ❑ rain jacket and pants
- ❑ sandals to wear around camp and to ford streams
- ❑ sleeping bag
- ❑ waterproof stuff sack
- ❑ sleeping pad
- ❑ small bath towel
- ❑ stove and fuel
- ❑ tent
- ❑ toiletry items
- ❑ water filter
- ❑ whistle

With the outdoor market currently flooded with products, many of which are pure gimmickry, it seems impossible to both differentiate and choose. Do I really need a tropical fish–lined collapsible shower? (No, you don't.) The only defense against the maddening quantity of items thrust in your face is to think practically—and to do so before you go shopping. The worst buys are impulsive buys. Since most name brands will differ only slightly in quality, it's best to know what you're looking for in terms of function. Buy only what you need. You will, don't forget, be carrying what you've bought on your back. One hundred pounds of ultralight hiking gear is still one hundred pounds! Here are some things to keep in mind before you go shopping.

Clothes. Clothing is your armor against Mother Nature's little surprises. Hikers should be prepared for any possibility, especially when hiking in mountainous areas. Adequate rain protection and extra layers of clothing are a good idea. In summer, a wide-brimmed hat is essential in the desert. In the winter months the first layer you'll want to wear is a "wicking" layer of long underwear that keeps perspiration away from your skin. Wear long underwear made from synthetic fibers that wick moisture away from the skin and draw it toward the next layer of clothing, where it then evaporates. Avoid wearing long underwear made of cotton, as it is slow to dry and keeps moisture next to your skin.

The second layer you'll wear is the "insulating" layer. Aside from keeping you warm, this layer needs to "breathe" so you stay dry while hiking. A fabric that provides insulation and dries quickly is fleece. It's interesting to note that this one-of-a-kind fabric is made out of recycled plastic. Purchasing a zip-up jacket made of this material is highly recommended.

The last line of layering defense is the "shell" layer. You'll need some type of waterproof, windproof, breathable jacket that will fit over all of your other layers. It should have a large hood that fits over a hat. You'll also need a good pair of rain pants made from a similar waterproof, breathable fabric, such as Gore-Tex or one of the alternatives.

Now that you've learned the basics of layering, you can't forget to protect your hands and face. In cold, windy, or rainy weather you'll need a hat made of wool or fleece and insulated, waterproof gloves that will keep your hands warm and toasty. As mentioned earlier, buying an additional pair of light silk liners to wear under your regular gloves is a good idea.

Footwear. If you have any extra money to spend on your trip, put that money into boots or trail shoes. Poor shoes will bring a hike to a halt faster than anything else. To avoid this annoyance, buy shoes that provide support and are lightweight and flexible. A lightweight hiking boot is better than a heavy, leather mountaineering boot for most day hikes and backpacking. Trail running shoes provide a little extra cushion and are made in a high-top style that many people wear for hiking. These running shoes are lighter, more flexible, and more breathable than hiking boots. If you know you'll be hiking in wet weather often, purchase boots or shoes with a Gore-Tex or equivalent waterproof and breathable liner, which will help keep your feet dry.

When buying your hiking shoes, be sure to wear the same type of socks you'll be wearing on the trail. If the boots you're buying are for cold weather hiking, try the boots on while wearing two pairs of socks. Speaking of socks, a good cold weather sock combination is to wear a thinner sock made of wool or polypropylene covered by a heavier outer sock made of wool or a synthetic/wool mix. The inner sock protects the foot from the rubbing effects of the outer sock and prevents blisters. Many outdoor stores have some type of ramp to simulate hiking uphill and downhill. Be sure to take advantage of this test, as toe-jamming boot fronts can be very painful and debilitating on the downhill trek.

Once you've purchased your footwear, be sure to break them in before you hit the trail. New footwear is often stiff and needs to be stretched and molded to your foot.

Hiking poles. Hiking poles help with balance and, more importantly, take pressure off your knees. The ones with shock absorbers are easier on your elbows and knees. Some poles even come with a camera attachment to be used as a monopod. And heaven forbid you meet a mountain lion, bear, or unfriendly dog, the poles can make you look a lot bigger. Some people prefer a single walking stick, because it's easier to free up your hands for activities such as rock scrambling and photography. A walking stick or trekking poles can also be used as a tarp support in the treeless desert, saving the weight of poles. In either case, make sure your stick or poles have rubber, not metal tips. In the rocky desert, rubber grips are much better than metal and far quieter.

Backpacks. No matter what type of hiking you do, you'll need a pack of some sort to carry the basic trail essentials. There are a variety of backpacks on the market, but let's first discuss what you intend to use it for. Day hikes or overnight trips?

If you plan on doing a day hike, a daypack should have some of the following characteristics: a padded hip belt that's at least 2 inches in diameter (avoid packs with only a small nylon piece of webbing for a hip belt); a chest strap (the chest strap helps stabilize the pack against your body); external pockets to carry items that you want easy access to; an internal pocket to hold keys, a knife, a wallet, and other miscellaneous items; an external lashing system to hold a jacket; and, if you so desire, a hydration pocket for carrying a hydration system (which consists of a water bladder with an attachable drinking hose). In the desert, don't put water bottles in outside pockets—the sun will quickly heat the water. Instead, put your bottles inside your pack under a jacket or other insulation.

For short hikes, some hikers like to use a fanny pack to store just a camera, food, a compass, a map, and other trail essentials. Most fanny packs have pockets for two water bottles and a padded hip belt. But fanny packs can't carry the gear needed to safely do longer or remoter hikes.

If you intend to do an extended, overnight trip, there are multiple considerations. First off, you need to decide what kind of framed pack you want. There are two backpack types for backpacking: the internal frame and the external frame. An internal frame pack rests closer to your body, making it more stable and easier to balance when hiking over rough terrain, a consideration if you like to hike remote, rough trails or cross-country. An external frame pack is just that, an aluminum frame attached to the exterior of the pack. Some hikers consider an external frame pack to be better for long backpack trips because it distributes the pack weight better and allows you to carry heavier loads. It's often easier to pack, and your gear is more accessible. It also offers better back ventilation in the desert.

The most critical measurement for fitting a pack is torso length. The pack needs to rest evenly on your hips without sagging. A good pack will come in two or three sizes and have straps and hip belts that are adjustable according to your body size and characteristics.

When you purchase a backpack, go to an outdoor store with salespeople who are knowledgeable in how to properly fit a pack. Once the pack is fitted for you, load the pack with the amount of weight you plan on taking on the trail. (Extra water bottles can substitute for heavy items such as food.) The weight of the pack should be distributed evenly, and you should be able to swing your arms and walk briskly without feeling out of balance. Another good technique for evaluating a pack is to walk up and down stairs and make quick turns to the right and to the left to be sure the pack doesn't feel out of balance. Other features that are nice to have on a backpack include a removable daypack or fanny pack, external pockets for items that need to be handy, and extra lash points to attach a jacket or other items. However, avoid getting a pack that is too small. You'll end up lashing gear to the outside, where it puts you off-balance and catches on brush and tree limbs.

Sleeping bags and pads. Sleeping bags are more or less rated by temperature. You can purchase a bag made with synthetic insulation, or you can buy a goose down bag. Goose down bags are more expensive, but they have a higher insulating capacity by weight and will keep their loft longer. You'll want to purchase a bag with a temperature rating that fits the time of year and conditions you are most likely to camp in. One caveat: The techno-standard for temperature ratings is far from perfect. Ratings vary from manufacturer to manufacturer, so to protect yourself you should purchase a bag rated 10 to 15 degrees below the temperature you expect to be camping in. Synthetic bags are more resistant to water than down bags, but most down bags are now made with down that is treated to make it highly water repellent. Down bags are also more compressible than synthetic bags and take up less room in your pack, which is an important consideration if you are planning a multiday backpack trip. Features to look for in a sleeping bag include a mummy style bag, a hood you can cinch down around your head in cold weather, and draft tubes along the zippers that help keep heat in and drafts out.

You'll also want a sleeping pad to provide insulation and padding from the cold ground. There are different types of sleeping pads available, from the more expensive self-inflating air mattresses to the less expensive closed-cell foam pads. Self-inflating air mattresses are usually heavier than closed-cell foam mattresses and are prone to punctures, especially in cactus country.

Tents. The tent is your home away from home while on the trail. It provides protection from wind, rain, snow, and insects. A three-season tent with a separate waterproof fly is a good choice for backpacking and can range in price from $100 to $500. A tent with net panels in the canopy provides more ventilation and is more comfortable in the desert. These lightweight and versatile tents provide protection in all types of weather, except heavy snowstorms or high winds, and range in weight from four to eight pounds. Look for a tent that's easy to set up and will easily fit two people with gear. Dome type tents usually offer more headroom and places to store gear. Other handy tent features include a vestibule where you can store wet boots and backpacks. Some nice-to-have items in a tent include interior pockets to store small items and lashing points to hang a clothesline. Even if your tent is completely self-supporting, always stake it securely so that it doesn't blow away in the wind while you're outside enjoying the sunset. Before you purchase a tent, set it up and take it down a few times to be sure it is easy to handle. Also, sit inside the tent and make sure it has enough room for you and your gear.

Cell phones. Many hikers are carrying their cell phones into the backcountry these days in case of emergency. That's fine and good, but please know that cell phone coverage is often poor to nonexistent in valleys, canyons, and thick forest. The companies providing cell phone coverage build towers where the customers are: cities and major highways. Coverage in wilderness areas is incidental to their business model. More importantly, people have started to call for help because they're just tired and don't feel like hiking out. Let's go back to being prepared. You are responsible for yourself in the backcountry—which is one of the major attractions of being a hiker! Use your brain to avoid problems, and if you do encounter one, first use your brain to try to correct the situation. Only use your cell phone, if it works, in true emergencies. If it doesn't work down low in a valley, try hiking to a high point where you might get reception.

Hiking with Children

Hiking with children isn't a matter of how many miles you can cover or how much elevation gain you make in a day; it's about seeing and experiencing nature through their eyes.

Kids like to explore and have fun. They like to stop and point out bugs and plants, look under rocks, jump in puddles, and throw sticks. If you're taking a toddler or young child on a hike, start with a trail that you're familiar with. Trails that have interesting things for kids, like piles of leaves to play in or a small stream to wade through during the summer, will make the hike much more enjoyable for them and will keep them from getting bored.

You can keep your child's attention if you have a strategy before starting on the trail. Using games is not only an effective way to keep a child's attention, it's also a great way to teach him or her about nature. Quiz children on the names of plants and animals. Pick up a family-friendly outdoor hobby like geocaching (www .geocaching .com) or letterboxing (www.atlasquest.com), both of which combine the outdoors, clue-solving, and treasure hunting. If your children are old enough, let them carry their own daypack filled with snacks and water. So that you are sure to go at their pace and not yours, let them lead the way. Playing follow the leader works particularly well when you have a group of children. Have each child take a turn at being the leader.

With children, a lot of clothing is key. The only thing predictable about weather is that it will change. Especially in mountainous areas, weather can change dramatically in a very short time. Always bring extra clothing for children, regardless of the season. In the winter, have your children wear wool socks and warm layers such as long underwear, a fleece jacket and hat, wool mittens, and good rain gear. It's not a bad idea to have these along in late fall and early spring as well. Good footwear is also important. A sturdy pair of high-top tennis shoes or lightweight hiking boots are the best bet for little ones. If you're hiking in the summer near a lake or stream, bring along a pair of old sneakers that your child can put on when he wants to go exploring in the water. Remember when you're near any type of water, always watch your child at all times. Also, keep a close eye on teething toddlers who may decide a rock or a leaf of poison oak is an interesting item to put in their mouth.

From spring through fall, you'll want your kids to wear a wide-brimmed hat to keep their face, head, and ears protected from the hot sun. Also, make sure your children wear sunscreen at all times. Choose a brand without PABA—children have sensitive skin and may have an allergic reaction to sunscreen that contains PABA. If you are hiking with a child younger than six months, don't use sunscreen or insect repellent. Instead, be sure that their head, face, neck, and ears are protected from the sun with a wide-brimmed hat, and that all other skin exposed to the sun is protected with the appropriate clothing.

Remember that food is fun. Kids like snacks, so it's important to bring a lot of munchies for the trail. Stopping often for snack breaks is a fun way to keep the trail interesting. Raisins, apples, granola bars, crackers and cheese, cereal, and trail mix all make great snacks. Also, a few of their favorite candy treats can go a long way toward heading off a fit of fussing. If your child is old enough to carry his or her own backpack, let him or her fill it with some lightweight "comfort" items such as a doll, a small stuffed animal, or a little toy (you'll have to draw the line at bringing the ten-pound Tonka truck). If your kids don't like drinking water, you can bring some powdered drink mix or a juice box.

Avoid poorly designed child-carrying packs—you don't want to break your back carrying your child. Most child-carrying backpacks designed to hold a forty-pound child will contain a large carrying pocket to hold diapers and other items. Some have an optional rain/sun hood.

Bringing your furry friend with you is always more fun than leaving him behind. Our canine pals make great trail buddies because they never complain and always make good company. Hiking with your dog can be a rewarding experience, especially if you plan ahead.

Getting your dog in shape. Before you plan outdoor adventures with your dog, make sure he's in shape for the trail. Getting your dog into shape takes the same discipline as getting yourself into shape, but luckily your dog can get in shape with you. Take your dog with you on your daily runs or walks. If there is a park near your house, hit a tennis ball or play Frisbee with your dog.

Swimming is also an excellent way to get your dog into shape. If there is a lake or river near where you live and your dog likes the water, have him retrieve a tennis ball or stick. Gradually build your dog's stamina up over a two- to three-month period. A good rule of thumb is to assume that your dog will travel twice as far as you will on the trail. If you plan on doing a 5-mile hike, be sure your dog is in shape for a 10-mile hike.

Training your dog for the trail. Before you go on your first hiking adventure with your dog, be sure he has a firm grasp on the basics of canine etiquette and behavior. Make sure he can sit, lie down, stay, and come. One of the most important commands you can teach your canine pal is to "come" under any situation. It's easy for your friend's nose to lead him astray or possibly get lost. Another helpful command is the "get behind" command. When you're on a hiking trail that's narrow, you can have your dog follow behind you when other trail users approach. Nothing is more bothersome than an enthusiastic dog that runs back and forth on the trail and disrupts the peace of the trail for others—or, worse, jumps up on other hikers and gets them muddy. Remember that some people have had bad experiences with dogs and are frightened when a dog approaches or jumps up on them. When you see other trail users approaching you on the trail, give them the right-of-way by quietly stepping off the trail and making your dog lie down and stay until they pass.

Equipment. The most critical pieces of equipment you can invest in for your dog are proper identification and a sturdy leash. Flexi-leads work well for hiking because they give your dog more freedom to explore but still leave you in control. (Some areas restrict the length of leashes—Valley of Fire State Park restricts leashes to 6 feet.) Make sure your dog has identification that includes your name and address and a number for your veterinarian. Other forms of identification for your dog include a tattoo or a microchip. You should consult your veterinarian for more information on these last two options.

The next piece of equipment you'll want to consider is a pack for your dog. By no means should you hold all of your dog's essentials in your pack—let him carry his own gear! Dogs that are in good shape can carry 30 to 40 percent of their own weight.

Most packs are fitted by a dog's weight and girth measurement. Companies that make dog packs generally include guidelines to help you pick out the size that's right for your dog. Some characteristics to look for when purchasing a pack for your dog include a harness that contains two padded girth straps, a padded chest strap, leash attachments, removable saddlebags, internal water bladders, and external gear cords.

You can introduce your dog to the pack by first placing the empty pack on his back and letting him wear it around the yard. Keep an eye on him during this first introduction. He may decide to chew through the straps if you aren't watching him closely. Once he learns to treat the pack as an object of fun and not a foreign enemy, fill the pack evenly on both sides with a few ounces of dog food in resealable plastic bags. Have your dog wear his pack on your daily walks for a period of two to three weeks. Each week add a little more weight to the pack until your dog will accept carrying the maximum amount of weight he can carry.

You can also purchase collapsible water and dog food bowls for your dog. These bowls are lightweight and can easily be stashed into your pack or your dog's. If you are hiking on rocky terrain or in the snow, you can purchase footwear for your dog that will protect his feet from cuts and bruises.

Always carry plastic bags to remove feces from the trail. It is a courtesy to other trail users and helps protect local wildlife.

The following is a list of items to bring when you take your dog hiking: collapsible water bowls, a comb, a collar and a leash, dog food, plastic bags for feces, a dog pack, flea/tick powder, paw protection, water, and a first-aid kit that contains eye ointment, tweezers, scissors, stretchy foot wrap, gauze, antibacterial wash, sterile cotton tip applicators, antibiotic ointment, and cotton wrap.

First aid for your dog. Your dog is just as prone—if not more prone—to getting in trouble on the trail as you are, so be prepared. Here's a rundown of the more likely misfortunes that might befall your little friend.

Bees and wasps. If a bee or wasp stings your dog, remove the stinger with a pair of tweezers and place a mudpack or a cloth dipped in cold water over the affected area. If you spot bees, especially a swarm, keep your dog on a leash and close to you because of the danger from Africanized bees. Dogs are commonly killed when they disturb Africanized bees, and the bees may attack you too.

Porcupines. One good reason to keep your dog on a leash is to prevent it from getting a nose full of porcupine quills. You may be able to remove the quills with pliers, but a veterinarian is the best person to do this nasty job because most dogs need to be sedated.

Heat stroke. Avoid hiking with your dog in really hot weather. Dogs with heat stroke will pant excessively, lie down and refuse to get up, and become lethargic and disoriented. If your dog shows any of these signs on the trail, have him lie down in the shade. If you are near a stream, pour cool water over your dog's entire body to help bring his body temperature back to normal.

Heartworm. Dogs get heartworm from mosquitoes which carry the disease in the prime mosquito months of July and August. Giving your dog a monthly pill prescribed by your veterinarian easily prevents this condition.

Plant pitfalls. One of the biggest plant hazards for dogs on the trail are foxtails. Foxtails are pointed grass seed heads that bury themselves in your friend's fur, between his toes, and even get in his ear canal. If left unattended, these nasty seeds can work their way under the skin and cause abscesses and other problems. If you have a long-haired dog, consider trimming the hair between his toes and giving him a summer haircut to help prevent foxtails from attaching to his fur. After every hike, always look over your dog for these seeds—especially between his toes and his ears.

Other plant hazards include burrs, thorns, thistles, and poison oak. If you find any burrs or thistles on your dog, remove them as soon as possible before they become an unmanageable mat. Thorns can pierce a dog's foot and cause a great deal of pain. If you see that your dog is lame, stop and check his feet for thorns. Dogs are immune to poison oak, but they can pick up the sticky, oily substance from the plant and transfer it to you.

Protect those paws. Be sure to keep your dog's nails trimmed so he avoids getting soft tissue or joint injuries. If your dog slows and refuses to go on, check to see that his paws aren't torn or worn. You can protect your dog's paws from trail hazards such as sharp gravel, foxtails, lava scree, and thorns by purchasing dog boots.

Sunburn. If your dog has light skin, he is an easy target for sunburn on his nose and other exposed skin areas. You can apply a nontoxic sunscreen to exposed skin areas that will help protect him from overexposure to the sun.

Ticks and fleas. Ticks can easily give your dog Lyme disease, as well as other diseases. Before you hit the trail, treat your dog with a flea and tick spray or powder. You can also ask your veterinarian about a once-a-month pour-on treatment that repels fleas and ticks.

Mosquitoes and deerflies. These little flying machines can do a job on your dog's snout and ears. Best bet is to spray your dog with fly repellent for horses to discourage both pests.

Giardia. Dogs can get giardia, which results in diarrhea. It is usually not debilitating, but it's definitely messy. A vaccine against giardia is available.

Mushrooms. Make sure your dog doesn't sample mushrooms along the trail. They could be poisonous to him, but he doesn't know that.

When you are finally ready to hit the trail with your dog, keep in mind that national parks and many wilderness areas do not allow dogs on trails. Your best bet is to hike in national forests, BLM lands, and state parks. Always call ahead to see what the restrictions are.

Further Reading

Fletcher, Colin. *The Complete Walker*. New York: Knopf, 2002.

Grayson, Donald K. *The Desert's Past*. Washington, DC: Smithsonian Institution Press, 1993.

Jacobson, Cliff. *Basic Illustrated Map and Compass*. Guilford, CT: Globe Pequot Press, 2008.

Larson, Peggy, and Lane Larson. *The Deserts of the Southwest*. San Francisco: Sierra Club Books, 1990.

Trimble, Stephen. *The Sagebrush Ocean*. Reno: University of Nevada Press, 1989.

Wuerthner, George. *Nevada Mountain Ranges*. Helena, MT: American and World Geographic Publishing, 1992.

Clubs and Trail Groups

Las Vegas Mountaineers Club, https://lvmc.org

Sierra Club, Toiyabe Chapter, PO Box 8096, Reno 89507; www.sierraclub.org/toiyabe

Hike Index

About the Author

Bruce Grubbs has a serious problem: He doesn't know what he wants to do when he grows up. Meanwhile, he's done such things as wildland firefighting, running a mountain shop, flying airplanes, shooting photos, and writing books. He's a back-country skier, climber, figure skater, mountain biker, amateur radio operator, river runner, and sea kayaker—but the thing that really floats his boat is hiking and back-packing. No matter what else he tries, the author always come back to hiking—especially long, rough, cross-country trips in places like the Grand Canyon. Some people never learn. But what little he has learned, he's willing share with you—via his books, of course, but also via his website, blogs, and whatever else works. His website is BruceGrubbs.com.

THE TEN ESSENTIALS OF HIKING

American Hiking Society

American Hiking Society recommends you pack the "Ten Essentials" every time you head out for a hike. Whether you plan to be gone for a couple of hours or several months, make sure to pack these items. Become familiar with these items and know how to use them. Learn more at **AmericanHiking.org/hiking-resources**

1. Appropriate Footwear

6. Safety Items (light, fire, and a whistle)

2. Navigation

7. First Aid Kit

3. Water (and a way to purify it)

8. Knife or Multi-Tool

4. Food

9. Sun Protection

5. Rain Gear & Dry-Fast Layers

10. Shelter

PROTECT THE PLACES YOU LOVE TO HIKE

Become a member today and take $5 off an annual membership using the code **Falcon5**.

AmericanHiking.org/join

American Hiking Society is the only national nonprofit organization dedicated to empowering all to enjoy, share, and preserve the hiking experience.